Memories of UNION HIGH

An Oasis in
Caroline County, Virginia
1903–1969

Memories of
UNION HIGH

An Oasis in
Caroline County, Virginia
1903–1969

MARION WOODFORK SIMMONS

Woodfork Genealogy LLC

Burtonsville, Maryland

Printed in the United States of America

First Edition: September 2011
ISBN 978-0-615-53092-5
Library of Congress Control Number: 2011915404

Woodfork Genealogy LLC
Burtonsville, Maryland

http://www.woodforkgenealogy.com

DEDICATION

In memory of my mother, Dorothy L. Woodfork (1926 – 2008), who encouraged my love of learning with weekly trips to the library and outings to museums, theaters, and many other cultural events. She also piqued my interest in genealogy and local history by sharing her photo albums, memorabilia and memories of growing up in Washington, D.C.

TABLE OF CONTENTS

TABLE OF CONTENTS

AUTHOR'S NOTES

It may be useful for readers to review Appendix B—Historical Background before reading the book to understand the historical events that took place during the time period it covers.

Grammar, spelling, and punctuation have been standardized for ease of reading when passages from yearbooks, articles, or other original materials were transcribed.

Over the years, a variety of racial classifications have been used to describe Americans of African descent: Negro, Colored, Black, and African American. The racial classifications used in this book reflect the term that was in use during the time period being discussed.

PREFACE

While performing genealogy research in 2004, I learned that my great grandfather, Overton Roy Woodfork, left Caroline County, Virginia, in the late 1800s and moved to Washington, D.C. I began to travel to the county for genealogy research. I noticed a dearth of information about African Americans in many of the libraries and historical archives. As I talked to African Americans in the county, however, I would hear interesting stories of their lives growing up in Caroline County. They would often mention the Caroline Sunday School Union and the organization's efforts to educate the African American children by building and supporting more than 30 one- and two-room school houses, as well as a secondary school. The secondary school eventually became part of the Caroline County school system and was the only high school for Negro children during segregation. People often spoke with pride about the dedicated administration, the nurturing teachers, and the students' desire to excel. Alumni had fond memories of participating in clubs and sports teams, traveling on field trips, and attending many school functions.

As I listened to their stories, I would often think what interesting information it was and that someone should preserve it. In 2009, I decided to become that someone. Originally, I planned to write a book on all the school houses and schools (Black and White) in Caroline County. But I soon realized the scope of the project was much too large, so I narrowed it down to Union High School. Thus, the Union High History Project was born.

The purpose of the Union High History Project was to research, document, and preserve the history of Union High School. Information was gathered from a variety of sources, including libraries, historical archives, newspapers, and books. Various methods were used to locate Union High alumni, faculty, family, and friends, including articles in the county's two newspapers (*Free Lance Star* and *Caroline Progress*), radio announcements, letters to the African American churches in the county, the Caroline Sunday School Union, the Union High Reunion Committee, and libraries in Caroline County and the nearby areas. Union High alumni, faculty, family, and friends were interviewed and their memories documented. They also shared their school memorabilia such as yearbooks, photographs, and other school documents.

This book is the end result of the Union High History Project. My goal was to create a work that preserved the history of the school and served as a memory book for those who were associated with the school. It is my sincere hope that the book does justice to the legacy of "Dear Old Union High."

ACKNOWLEDGEMENTS

This book is the result of contributions from many people. I have tried to list everyone, but if I missed a name, please know that your contribution and support are greatly appreciated.

Union High alumni, faculty, family, and friends who generously shared their knowledge, memories, and memorabilia. Without their participation, this book would not have been possible. Appendix C contains a list of the Union High History Project participants.

Caroline County Angels—As part of The Papers of Archie G. Richardson 1918–1976 in the Special Collections and Archives of the Johnston Memorial Library of Virginia State University are pages and pages of notes about the Negro community in Caroline County, Virginia. These notes are not dated and do not contain any information about the author(s). However, they appear to have been written during the 1940s or early 1950s by several residents from Caroline County. I called these unknown people my Caroline County Angels and greatly appreciate their efforts to preserve a portion of the county's history.

Mr. Gilbert Brittle Jr., president of the Caroline Historical Society, for sharing his notes of the Caroline County School Board meeting minutes and his knowledge of the Caroline school system.

Ms. Kay Brooks and the staff of the Caroline Library.

The staff of the Central Rappahannock Heritage Central Library.

Mr. Ray S. Campbell, court clerk, and all the staff at the Caroline County circuit court.

Ms. Mary S. Clark, director, Acquisitions and Access Management, The Library of Virginia.

Mr. Lucious Edwards and the staff of the Special Collections and Archives, Johnston Memorial Library, Virginia State University.

Mr. Patrick Ellis and WHUR Radio for spreading the word about the Union High History Project.

Ms. Edie Gross for writing an article on the project in the *Free Lance Star* and providing me with pertinent news articles from the *Free Lance Star* archive.

Rev. Carroll Jackson and the members of the Caroline Sunday School Union.

Mr. Dave Klausner (pixlfixl.com) for photo restoration

Ms. Diana McCain, head of the Research Center, The Connecticut Historical Society, Hartford, Connecticut.

Mr. David Overton for designing the cover and laying out the book.

Ms. Donzella Maupin and the staff of the Hampton University, University Archives.

Ms. Marie Morton and the staff of Paciulli, Simmons & Associates, Ltd.; working with you on the AP Hill Oral History Project gave me the inspiration for the Union High History Project.

Mr. Bob Sardelli for photo restoration.

Ms. Barbie Selby, University of Virginia, Alderman Library Reference, University of Virginia.

Ms. Jane Sevier, for editing my manuscript and helping transform it to the polished finished product.

Mr. Ed Simmons Jr. for writing a news article about the project in the *Caroline Progress*.

Ms. Gloria Simpson and the Union High School Reunion Committee for sending letters to Union High alumni and helping spread the word about the project.

Last but not least, my husband, daughters, friends, and other well-wishers who provided me with encouragement and moral support throughout this project.

Introduction

Union High School began as a private secondary school (Bowling Green Industrial Academy) in Caroline County, Virginia. It was established and supported by the Caroline Sunday School Union to provide the Negro children in the community with more than a rudimentary education. It later became a training school for Negro teachers (Caroline County Training School) and finally a four-year accredited public high school (Union High School). It was the only source of secondary education for Negro children in Caroline County during the era of segregation.

Most of the information published about the education of Negro children during this era has focused on the dismal conditions of the facilities and the inferior education the children received. It is true that during segregation Negro schools received far less funding and resources than White schools, Negro teachers were paid must less than their White counterparts, and school boards were less receptive to requests from Negro parents. But a positive aspect of these segregated schools is often overlooked.

Union High alumni, like many alumni of segregated schools, speak fondly of their school. With church and home, it was an important institution in their community. Adults worked very hard to provide their children with opportunities to ensure they would have a better life. Education was seen as the key to a better future for the children, the community, and the race.

Alumni often refer to Union High as being like a family. The administration and faculty nurtured, supported, and encouraged the students. They held them to high standards and expected to them to excel; failure was not an option. Parents and members of the community strove to support the school in every way possible. And the school served all members of the community, not just students. For many, Union High was an oasis that sheltered them from the hardships of growing up in a segregated society and provided them a solid foundation to become productive members of society.

The Vision

On November 21, 1898, Rev. R. B. Fortune, E. A. Johnson, James Baylor, George Lonesome, and R. W. Young, trustees of the Sunday School Union of the Baptist Colored People of Caroline County, purchased 19 1/4 acres of land in Bowling Green, Virginia, from Joseph and Estella Degler for $300. The property was to be held for "the purpose of establishing an Industrial Academy for the Colored people under the auspices and control of the Sunday School Union." [1] With this purchase, the Sunday School Union led by Rev. Young put in motion its plans to provide secondary education for the Negro children of Caroline County.

Establishing a secondary school was the brainchild of Rev. Young, president of the Union. The Caroline Sunday School Union was formed circa 1892 by Rev. J. H. Turner, pastor of the Shiloh Baptist Church in Bowling Green. [2] The purpose of the organization was to improve the religious life of the Negroes in Caroline County by encouraging them to use Bibles in Sunday School.

In 1894, Rev. Turner resigned from his church and left the county to become a pastor in another location. After his departure, the work of the Sunday School Union began to falter. Its membership dwindled from eight Sunday schools to two, and the treasury was depleted to $3.56. [3] Several members asked Rev. Young, pastor of the First Mount Zion and Ebenezer Baptist Churches, to assume the presidency. He agreed to take the position on one condition: the Sunday School Union must agree to build and operate a secondary school for the county's Negro children.

The officers of the Sunday School Union agreed to Rev. Young's condition and elected him as the second president in December 1895. [4] Under his leadership, the Sunday School Union worked diligently to increase its membership, replenish the treasury, and make their vision of providing educational opportunities to their children a reality.

In 1898, the Sunday School Union became interested in purchasing land on the outskirts of Bowling Green to use as the site for the school, but there was not enough money in the treasury. To move forward with the plans to establish the school, several members of the Sunday School Union agreed to secure a loan to obtain the funds necessary for the purchase. The Sunday School Union agreed to raise the money and repay the loan. On November 19, 1898, Rev. Johnson, Baylor, Fortune, Lonesome, and Young used their personal property as collateral to secure a loan from M. W. Beazley. [5] They purchased the property two days later.

The Sunday School Union members worked together to raise money and pay off the debt. On one occasion, a fundraising contest was held between the Sunday schools, and the school that raised the largest amount of money received a banner. The contest raised $215.92, and the Shiloh School in Bowling Green won the banner. [6]

After the loan from Beazley was repaid, the Sunday School Union focused on obtaining materials to construct the school. On August 27, 1901, Fortune, Johnson, Baylor, Lonesome, and Young, trustees for the Industrial Academy for Colored People, used the land as collateral to obtain a loan of $200 from O. P. Smoot. [7] That money was used to purchase building materials. By the fall of 1903 the first building—a wood-frame structure consisting of a girl's dormitory, classrooms, and a chapel—was near completion. It was named Young Hall in honor of Rev. R. W. Young. [8]

Bowling Green Industrial Academy (1903–1914)

On October 5, 1903, the Bowling Green Industrial Academy opened in a partially completed building as a private school with 5 students and 1 teacher.[9] Liston Leander Davis, an 1888 graduate of the Hampton Normal and Agricultural Institute (now Hampton University), was the principal and vocational education teacher. By January 1904, the enrollment had increased to 35 and 1 additional teacher, Nettie C. Bagby.[10]

The Academy received its charter from the State Corporation Commission of Virginia on April 21, 1904.[11] The main purpose of the corporation was "the Literary and Industrial Education of Colored youth of both sexes."[12] A board of trustees was established to manage its affairs. Members of the first board were: R. W. Young, president; W. G. Young, clerk; R. B. Fortune, treasurer; T. M. Allen; E. A. Johnson; James Baylor; George Lonesome; L. L. Davis; J.M. Beverly; W. L. Davis; W. J. Young; M. W. Wright. The first five were directors.[13] Board members were also members of the Sunday School Union.

The Board of Trustees paid all the expenses associated with operating the Academy, including the cost of instruction, facility upkeep, and room and board for the students. They also purchased more land to expand the campus. Five acres were acquired from James W. Gatewood on September 9, 1904, for $500.[14] Another 7 3/4 acres of land were brought from Luther and Sallie Scott

Liston Leander Davis, Principal, Bowling Green Industrial Academy.
SOURCE: *1969 UNION HIGH YEARBOOK.*

Rev. R. W. Young, Second President, Caroline Sunday School Union.
SOURCE: *THE HAMPTON UNIVERSITY ARCHIVES.*

on August 14, 1909, for $200.[15] These purchases made the total amount of property for the school campus approximately 32 acres.

The school was supported with financial and material contributions from churches, Sunday schools belonging to the Sunday School Union, and individuals from the Negro community. The school also received support from friends of all races outside the community such as Frances Matilda Wright from Nyron, North Carolina (originally from Wethersfield, Connecticut); Gertrude Warner of Wethersfield, Connecticut; and Annie E. Kemp from Flushing, New York.[16]

The school term was eight months (October through May). The curriculum was divided into four levels (Preparatory, Junior, Middle, and Senior) and consisted of both literary and industrial classes. There were several forms of extracurricular activities. Students participated in societies, organized by grade level, in which they learned to debate, conduct public meetings, and work in teams.[17] Boys were grouped into a company of cadets and drilled according to Upton's Tactics.[18] The objective was to teach them to be "courteous, prompt to obey, gentlemanly in bearing and self-control."[19] Boys could also participate in a drum and fife corps.

Bowling Green Industrial Academy was an integral part of Caroline County Negro community. Many of its graduates played a vital role in improving the quality of life in the community by becoming ministers and teachers.

By the 1911–1912 school year, the Academy had grown to include 82 students (43 elementary and 39 secondary) and 4 teachers.[20] It received $1,010 in income: $360 from tuition and $650 from other sources.[21] The Academy did not receive any state, federal, or municipal funds.

Members of the community sacrificed in many ways to provide educational opportunities for their children. Nannie Lee Butler, industrial supervising teacher in Caroline County, chronicled some of these sacrifices:

> One man whose property holdings are valued at only a thousand dollars and who has a growing family of eight to support gave out of his weekly earning in one year $250. How did he do it? Not all at once at some big rally. Sometimes at the freight office he would pay a bill for lime, cement, or other material, and at the next meeting of the School Improvement League, he would quietly hand the receipt to the treasurer.
>
> One man who did the mason work gave one-half of his time free. An-

other man who lives in a shabby, rented tenement contributed $5 of the $8 he had received for laying the cement floors of the porches. Still another man who did not have the ready money did have timber land, from which he cut and hauled logs to the mill and contributed the lumber cut from them.[22]

The rising cost associated with the Academy made it a constant struggle for the trustees to maintain the school. In 1913, they asked County Superintendent of Schools John Washington for financial assistance. Washington sought aid from the Slater Fund. The trustees agreed to turn over the school to the Caroline County School Board to receive money from the Slater Fund and establish a public secondary school for their children.

On October 28, 1914, the trustees donated 10 acres of land and the two school buildings estimated to be worth $2,500 to the Caroline County School Board.[23] Bowling Green Industrial Academy became part of the Caroline County public school system.

◄ *Bowling Green Industrial Academy class doing industrial work in 1912.*
COURTESY JACKSON DAVIS COLLECTION OF AFRICAN AMERICAN EDUCATIONAL PHOTOGRAPHS, SPECIAL COLLECTIONS, UNIVERSITY OF VIRGINIA LIBRARY.

Bowling Green Industrial Academy Industrial Exhibits ▶
COURTESY JACKSON DAVIS COLLECTION OF AFRICAN AMERICAN EDUCATIONAL PHOTOGRAPHS, SPECIAL COLLECTIONS, UNIVERSITY OF VIRGINIA LIBRARY.

Caroline County Training School (1914–1929)

When the Caroline County School Board assumed responsibility for the school, the name was changed to Caroline County Training School. George Hays Buchanan, a 1908 graduate of The Hampton Normal and Agricultural Institute (now Hampton University) and 1914 graduate of Lincoln University, was the principal. Rev. L. L. Davis continued as the agricultural teacher. The school was designed to train teachers for Negro schools by giving them seven years of elementary education and two additional years of teacher training. When they completed all nine grades, students were given a second-grade certificate that would allow them to teach. Because this was the lowest-level teaching certificate, students were encouraged to continue their education.[24]

Although the Caroline County School Board now owned the school, the Sunday School Union still remained responsible for operating and supporting it. The School Board provided the teachers and paid their salaries. The Sunday School Union was responsible for providing most of the fuel and was solely responsible for all room and board.

During the 1914–1915 school year, the total enrollment of the school was 212 students, and the faculty consisted of 4 teachers. The school comprised nine grades. The curriculum consisted of industrial work (cooking, sewing, manual training) and some gardening. The ninth-grade cur-

George Hayes Buchanan, 1914–1916
Courtesy Douglas Hayes Buchanan Sr.

A. M. Walker, 1916–1925.
Source: *Union High 1969 Yearbook*

riculum also included methods and management to prepare students to become teachers in rural schools. The total income for the school was $2,080: $1,430 from public funds, $500 from the Slater Fund, and $150 from other sources. Of the income received, $1,760 was used to pay teachers' salaries, and $320, for other purposes. The total value of the school plant was $4,300: 11 acres of land valued at $800, a six-room building valued at $2,000, and equipment valued at $1,500.[25]

In 1916, A. M. Walker—a graduate of the Virginia Normal Institute (now Virginia State University) in Petersburg, Virginia; Virginia Union University; and Howard University—became principal. The student population continued to increase, so much so that an additional building was needed. In 1921, a frame building was erected. The total cost for the new building was $9,000.[26] The funds for the building were obtained from the Rosenwald Fund ($1,600), money raised by the Sunday School Union ($2,400), and a gift to the Bowling Green Industrial Academy from the estate of Frances M. Wright ($5,000). All of the members of the Sunday School Union assisted in constructing the building. Even the principal worked on the evenings and Sunday to help complete the building.

Henry Morton Ruffin became the principal in 1925. Under his administration, a new auditorium would be built to replace the original one

Henry Morton Ruffin, 1925–1926.

Hovey Rice Young, 1926–1940.

that was built in 1903. Deacon R. B. Fortune organized the Caroline County-wide League to raise funds for the new building, which would be used as an auditorium and dormitory. Humphrey P. Latney, president of the Sunday School Union, and Principal H. M. Ruffin raised $300 for the project. One hundred dollars of the money was obtained from the county supervisors, and the other $200 was raised through a spade fund Latney created by using the spade that was used in the ground breaking for the new building.[27] Individuals and organizations raised the remaining funds. Ruffin resigned in the summer of 1926 when the building was completed.

Hovey Rice Young became principal in October 1926. His main goal was to have the school accredited as a four-year high school. During the 1928–1929 school year, Caroline County Training School qualified for accreditation from the Board of Education.[28] After the school qualified for accreditation, the principal and trustees felt the name should be changed to reflect the school's new status. Principal Young appointed a committee of faculty members to select a new name. Gertrude N. Young, a faculty member and wife of Rev. Andrew P. Young, suggested the name Union High to commemorate the work of the Sunday School Union.[29] The committee unanimously accepted the name and recommended the name change to the Caroline County School Board.

On June 3, 1929, the school board accepted the name change. They also recommended the school be placed on the list of accredited schools.[30] During the 1929–1930 school year, Union High qualified for accreditation from the board of education.[31] The following year, the school was accredited by the Virginia State Board of Education as a high school offering four-year courses in vocational agriculture.[32]

Caroline County Training School students, 9th and 10th grades, 1920s. Rev L. L. Davis is the first person on the left of the fourth row.

◀ *Unknown (left) and Zeddie Gatewood (right).* COURTESY YVONNE WOOLFOLK BRITTON.

(l. to r.) ▶ *Zeddie Gatewood, Ester Purse, Aquilla Brown.* COURTESY YVONNE WOOLFOLK BRITTON.

My mother, Zeddie Gatewood, was the daughter of Ham and Saberna Gatewood. She lived in Penola (now Ruther Glen). In order to get to school, she would take the train to Milford on Monday, stay in the dormitory during the week, and take the train home on Friday. During her senior year, she would ride with a classmate who had a car instead of taking the train. However, she would still stay in the dormitory during the week.

My mother enjoyed the time she spent at Caroline County Training School. One of her classmates was Jeremiah Alvesta Wright, the father of Rev. Jeremiah Wright Jr. [the former Pastor of the Trinity United Church of Christ (TUCC), in Chicago]. Her favorite teacher was Mrs. Naomi Miller. She graduated in 1929 and later married Julian V. Woolfolk, the son of Douglas and Virginia Woolfolk. She named her second daughter Naomi Miller Woolfolk in honor of her favorite teacher. My mother taught at Dawn Elementary School from 1929 to 1930. My mother and grandmother [Saberna Gatewood] were both teachers and very well respected in the community.

Yvonne Woolfolk Britton
Daughter of Zeddie Gatewood Woolfolk who graduated
from Caroline County Training School, Class of 1929

Caroline County Training School Class of 1929. (l. to. r.) Jeremiah Wright, Emma Shepard, Rosa Christopher, Louise Byrd, Dorothy Turner, Maudenia Harrison, Zeddie Gatewood, Esther Purce, Robert Saunders. COURTESY WESLEY T. CARTER.

Caroline County Training School, graduating class, May 19, 1921.
Laly Golden is the first person on the left in the back row.
COURTESY JACKSON DAVIS COLLECTION OF AFRICAN AMERICAN EDUCATIONAL PHOTOGRAPHS,
SPECIAL COLLECTIONS, UNIVERSITY OF VIRGINIA LIBRARY.

My mother [Laly Golden Davis] graduated from Caroline Training School in the 1920s. All the girls wore white dresses [at graduation] that they had made in domestic science class (later called home economics).

Marguerite Davis Jackson
Daughter of Laly Golden Davis

My mother, Viola Vergie Coleman, was very young when she started Caroline Training School. When she went to enroll, the principal was concerned about her having to stay in the dormitory. He said she was too young and would cry for her parents. My great aunt, Lillie Robinson, arranged for her to stay with Mr. Banks, who lived near the school. She moved into the dormitory after a short while when the principal realized she would be OK. She graduated in 1924 and was the class valedictorian. She attended Virginia Normal and Industrial Institute and graduated in 1928. She taught in Caroline County at Dawn (a one-room school house) and Cassia (a two-room school house). She was the first principal of the new Dawn Elementary that was built during consolidation. She retired in 1969 after teaching for 40 years and teaching three generations of students.

Evelyn Thomas Minor
Daughter of Viola Vergie Coleman Thomas
who graduated from Caroline County Training School; Class of 1924

Union High School (1929–1969)

At the start of the 1929–1930 school year, the hard work and perseverance of the members of the Sunday School Union and the Negro community in Caroline County finally paid off. For the first time, Negro children in the county had the opportunity to attend an accredited four-year public high school. The objectives of Union High were:

"To give to the Colored youth of the county such academic and industrial training as will enable those who desire higher work in teacher training or in college branches to do so without a serious handicap; to the multitudes that go no higher, proper ideals of home building and well rounded citizenship; and to all a keen appreciation of Christian character." [33]

There were 121 elementary students and 66 high school students.[34] The students were taught by 3 full-time elementary teachers, 4 full-time high school teachers, and 1 teacher who divided her time between the elementary and high school students. The principal taught four periods per day as well.[35]

In the early years, most communities had one- and two-room school houses where students received their elementary education. Union High had both elementary and high school grades, so Negro students in the Bowling Green community could continue in the same school for both their elementary and high school education. Negro students from other communi-

PHILOSOPHY

The School, to better aid the individual, should seek to unfold his natural tendencies rather than set up certain conventional and uniform standards of accomplishments, irrespective of ability. The points pertinent to guidance include social and civic behavior, loyalty to humanity, boy-girl relationships, and social hygiene. The best test for evaluating the school system is the appraisal society makes of the behavior of the School's product in the social situation encountered throughout life.

Learning takes place best when the pupil comes from a home in which the adults maintain a discipline conducive to study; when the child himself is intellectually normal by accepted standards; when his teachers are well qualified; when the school location is easily accessible; when the buildings and equipment are adequate; and when the Community offers no serious enticements towards juvenile delinquency. In addition, the accord between parent and teacher should be easy, the curriculum suitable, and the aims of the School thoroughly practical.

The institutions and individuals which should co-operate in the program of education should include the family, religious organizations, and civic and educational groups, as well as key individuals of the community. The School serves as an intellectual, informative and social hub of the community by being a place of important meetings, where programs of the best type are presented and where the most enlightened sentiment is created and set forth.

Education is the sum total of those measures taken by qualified institutions and persons to assist the student towards as happy a life as is possible in a changing civilization. Such assistance consists in helping the learner to attain the service of society.

The Administration

ties wishing to continue their education past the 7th grade had to travel to Bowling Green to attend Union High.

In 1947, Virginia switched from an 11-year school system to a 12-year system. Therefore, there is no class of 1951 because students starting the 8th grade in 1947 spent an additional year in high school and graduated in 1952.

Although Union High was a public high school, the administration, faculty, parents, and members of the community still had to fight to ensure the school received the same treatment as the White schools. The administration and faculty worked hard to make do with what they had been given. In the words of many Union High alumni, "They [the teachers] knew how to do a lot with a little." Clubs and organizations, athletic programs, and school functions supplemented the school's curriculum to broaden the student's horizons.

Overcrowding was a constant problem as the student population continued to grow each year. A new facility was built in 1952, and the building was enlarged three times over the next 12 years.

Although the facility provided more space, the school was unable to maintain a guidance and teaching staff large enough to meet the requirements for accreditation. As a result, several academic teachers taught more than the allowable number of class periods, and the class sizes exceeded the allowable number of students.[36] In 1967, the State Board of Education began to strictly enforce the standards for secondary schools to improve the quality of Virginia schools. On April 29, 1967, Union High was one of 36 schools warned by the State Board of Education that they were in danger of losing their accreditation. Union High addressed the deficiencies by hiring more teachers and another guidance counselor and was able to maintain its accreditation.

Changes came to Union High in 1964 when the Caroline County School Board implemented the Freedom of Choice program. A few students transferred to previously White high schools, and several White teachers joined the faculty. Five years later, the school ceased to exist when the Caroline County School system integrated.

Administration and Faculty

The administration and faculty were the heart and soul of Union High School. They did more than teach academics—they nurtured and cared for the students and worked hard to ensure they would become productive members of society.

Many administration and faculty had a passion for teaching. They saw their profession as a means to prepare the next generation to improve themselves, their community, and their race. The administration and faculty did not work under the best circumstances and often had to fight to receive the same treatment as the other schools.

Negro teachers were paid less than their White counterparts. For the 1930–1931 school year, the average salary for a white male high school teacher in Caroline County, Virginia, was $1,666, for a white female was $998, for a Negro male was $1,129, and for a Negro female was $668.[37] Negro teachers of Caroline County, like Negro teachers all over America, had to fight for the same pay as their White counterparts. They petitioned the Caroline School Board on March 7, 1938, and again on January 6, 1941, to ask for salary equalization.[38] No action was taken.[39] On March 16, 1942, the school board passed a resolution ordering equalization of salaries of White and Negro teachers over a three-year period effective July 1, 1942.[40]

George Brown Ruffin, principal 1940–1969.

George B. Ruffin, wife Gloria, and son Richard, 1962.

COURTESY PAULINE S. BOXLEY.

Teachers were very active in the community; they owned businesses, attended the churches, and were involved in many of the civic organizations. Many teachers taught multiple generations of a family. Some teachers also had students live with them from time to time. As a result of these frequent interactions, many teachers had well-established relationships with students and their parents. Many alumni remarked that their teachers become their surrogate parents when they were at school.

PRINCIPAL

George Brown Ruffin came to Union High school in 1937. He was hired to teach history, revive the athletic program, and coach baseball. He became the principal in 1940 after Hovey R. Young became ill. He held the position until 1969, when the school ceased to exist after the integration. Starting in 1952, Ruffin wrote a principal message to the students in the yearbook. These messages, located in Appendix A, give insight into his thoughts on education and student development.

Mr. Ruffin would give a student who did something wrong a demerit. Punishment was based on the number of demerits. For the first demerit, the student had to pick up trash around the school.

> *He lived for something. He did good and left behind him a monument of virtue that the storm of time can never destroy. He wrote his name in kindness, love, and mercy on the hearts of thousands he came in contact with year by year. He will never be forgotten. No, his name, his deeds will be as legible on the hearts he left behind as the stars on the brow of evening. Good deeds will shine as the stars of heaven.*
>
> **The Family**
>
> SOURCE: GEORGE BROWN RUFFIN FUNERAL PROGRAM

Second, you were not allowed to attend any school activities for a certain amount of time. Third, the student was sent home. No one wanted to be sent home because they would get in serious trouble with their parents. Students were rarely disruptive.

Principal Ruffin and his wife would visit the homes of students. They would have dinner with the student's family. The principal and teachers were like part of the family. Mr. Ruffin will long be remembered for his commitment, dedication, and service as our principal for more than thirty years.

Clara Latney Hudson
Class of 1949

Mr. Ruffin was very strict; he kept order in the school. If the boys were acting up, he would catch them by their ears and call them "rinky dinks."

Kate Hutchison Samuels
Class of 1950

Mr. Ruffin was tough and a strict disciplinarian. I was never sure if I lived up to his expectations until I had left school. In the late 1950s, I began my career at the Library of Congress. The Library had a Surplus Books Program from which books were made available to educational institutions. I notified Mr. Ruffin of the program, and he and Mr. Guss drove to D.C. to make selections for donation to Union High's library. When Mr. Ruffin came to my office, he seemed so proud that a Union High alumna was in that setting and able to help our school. It meant a lot to me to have made him proud and to have been of help to the school.

Emma Samuel Vaughan
Class of 1950

Mr. Ruffin tried to get the best from the students. He insisted on us doing our best. He was not just a principal; he was a disciplinarian, parent, and friend.

Vivian Garnett Coleman
Class of 1953

Mr. Ruffin was strict but fair. He was a teacher, principal, and father all together.

Dorothy Carter Black
Class of 1952

Mr. Ruffin was always in the hall. He was a big man and always had a smile on his face. Everyone respected him. He would tell me "Miss Collins, you better get in the classroom." He would call me into the office to look over my schedule to make sure I was taking the right courses.

Beulah Collins
Class of 1959

I will never forget the day my best girlfriend since elementary school, Louise Golden Coghill, and I decided that we needed to get our hair washed and curled because we were going to be in the school play given by the Dramatic Club, which we were members of and wanted to look cute. When we got off the [school]bus, we walked to Bowling Green because we could not get anyone to take us. Just as the hairdresser was finishing me, Mr. Ruffin our principal, walked in and said "Here are my two girls, I've been looking all over Bowling Green for you. Get in this car; I am taking you back to school." I was scared to death, shaking in my shoes, and so was my best friend Louise, who is now deceased. She passed in Dec. 2008. When we got back to school, he took us around to each classroom and explained to the teachers and students that we had gone to Bowling Green without permission to get our hair fried. That day was the most embarrassing day of my life at age 14. He sent a letter home to my mother by me. She reprimanded me all over again. You would have thought we had killed someone. Our punishment from Mr. Ruffin was that we had to bring wood in for the potbelly wood stoves for three weeks. That was called the chain gang and the only time I ever got in trouble in four years. We knew better than to break any rules after that.

Bert Twiggs Nichols
Class of 1948

DEDICATION

For having ceaselessly devoted your intellect, time and energy to the general welfare of humanity and more especially to the progress of Union High School, we the senior class proudly dedicate this annual to our principal. Mr. George Brown Ruffin.

At no time have we ever found you too busy to help us solve our problems. Never have we known you to be too heavy laden to inject a lifting word of humor nor unwilling to exert your efforts above and beyond the call of duty.

As a leader of men and a gentleman of honor, King and Queen County does itself proud to claim you as one of its native sons. As a brilliant scholar; the King and Queen Industrial High School where you received your early education, Virginia Union University where you earned the A. B. Degree, The University of Pennsylvania that conferred the M.A. Degree, and Ohio State College where you have continued your professional improvement, single you out with dignity as one of their illustrious alumnus. As the sixth principal of Union High School, where you served three years as history teacher and athletic coach, the students and people of Carolina laud these twenty-one years of progressive leadership as significant to their way of life.

Your radiant personality has not been contained within the boundaries of our County nor District. Successfully, you have manned the helm of the Secondary Principal's Group of the First District Teachers Association for twelve years as their president and chairman of their Study Group. Memories of your courageous exploits and victorious spirit on the athletic fields of various colleges aided the members of Virginia Union University National Panther Club to select you as their chaplain. The growth of the First District Teachers Association can be attributed in part to your participation as a member and vice president.

Our exhaustive labours on this annual fed our desires to dedicate it to some one who had sacrificed more than we. Our rich experiences at Union High will remain in the archives with those who have preceded us, and we wanted to dedicate this annual to someone who had worked with us more than they. Our high esteem led us to dedicate this Annual to you, Mr. George Brown Ruffin. May many more students be blessed by your guidance. and learn to serve humanity as worthwhile citizens through your exemplary life as principal. teacher, and friend.

SOURCE: *1958 UNION HIGH YEARBOOK*

In my sophomore year, I became discouraged and was going to drop out of school to join the military. Mr. Ruffin talked me out of it. He said, "If you don't have a high school diploma, they [the military] will not want you. If you do get in, they will not promote you."

Rev. Joseph Dobbins
Class of 1959

Mr. Ruffin was tough. He did not want anyone in the halls. He would monitor the halls. If a student was in the hall he would say, "Hey little fella, little lady!! Where are you going?" He was also nice. He took the senior class to his home to have a picnic toward the end of the year.

Nina Woolfolk Harley
Class of 1961

Mr. Ruffin was an authority figure and a disciplinarian. He was respected by the teachers and students. Most of the students were afraid of him. He knew everyone's parents and would come to the student's home. Mr. Ruffin was a magnificent person. He believed in education and wanted the students to be the best they could be. He taught us to be proud of what we had.

Barbara Jones Rock
Class of 1961

Mr. Ruffin required us to learn all four verses of the Negro National Anthem, "Lift Ev'ry Voice and Sing." He had us convinced that we had to learn them in order to graduate.

Patricia Sizer Adams
Class of 1964

Mr. Ruffin would make students wash the windows as punishment. If they did something very bad, he would put them in the car and take them [to their] home.

Rudolph Gray
Class of 1964

At first glance Mr. Ruffin looked mean and spoke rough; he ran a tight ship. Once you got to know him, he was a soft heart. He did not allow students to keep getting in trouble. If you got in trouble once, he made sure you did not get in trouble again. He would put students on his chain gang where they had to do work around the school like wash windows or clean the trophy case. He would make the boys trim the hedges or do any work that needed to be done around the school. You would get demerits [when you did something wrong], and the number of demerits determined how long you had to work on the chain gang. I never got demerits, so I only know about the chain gang from what other students told me.

Mr. Ruffin was an ally; he made sure the kids got what they needed. One day I was in the library and missed the school bus. Mr. Ruffin took me home. All the way home, he talked to me about my plans for life after high school: Was I going to college? Did I plan to work? etc. Questions I had never thought about.

Eleanor Thomas Hawkins
Class of 1965

Mr. Ruffin was a great principal. He was a serious, quiet, dignified man. He had a sense of humor, but his mere presence commanded respect. He wore a suit and tie everyday. He had two ways of calling students to the office over the intercom. One was routine. The other by the use of the word "immediately," with a certain tone, that let a student know he or she was in trouble.

Williabel Jones Davis
Class of 1966

Mr. Ruffin was always at the top of his game. He knew all the students by name. He was a caring person and a disciplinarian. When he called you to the office, you did not want to go. He would call students to the office over the intercom. I was called to the office once, "William Brawner, Joseph Courtney, and Jessie Stevens, report to the office IMMEDIATELY!!!" All the teachers were standing in their classroom doorways and shaking their heads as we walked by. When we got to the office, Mr. Ruffin said, "You little rascals!" He did not yell at us. He just talked to us about what we had done wrong. One of my buddies had taken a picture from a girl in our class without my awareness. We had to pick up trash around the school as our punishment.

William Brawner
Class of 1966

Mr. Ruffin commanded respect and gave respect. His stature alone commanded respect. He was a proud man, focused on education and discipline. He would remind you that he knew your parents and didn't hesitate to let them know what you were doing. His memory frightened me at times. Students really respected him and did not want to disappoint him.

Carolyn Garnett Epps
Class of 1966

Mr. Ruffin was well-respected and feared. Nobody wanted to be sent to the office. Someone would say, "Here comes Mr. Ruffin," and everyone would settle down. We did not want to get caught doing something we were not supposed to be doing.

Florence Lee Rhue
Class of 1965

Mr. Ruffin would start the morning announcements with, "Good Morning, Boys and Girls." He was a good disciplinarian and did not want students in the halls. Students would see him in the hall and say, "Here comes GB!!" He would catch the boys by their ears and take them to the office to give discipline. Punishment for minor things was to clean up around the school.

Regena Green Harris
Class of 1967

Mr. Ruffin encouraged the teachers to establish a relationship with the students and their parents. He encouraged them to attend the churches in the neighborhood and the Sunday School Union.

Jeanetta Rock Lee
Class of 1952
Secretary

Mr. Ruffin expected his teachers to be there, be on time, and be in class. He would walk around to see what was going on. He was very supportive.

Blonnie Tipton
Band Teacher

I came to Union High after graduating from Virginia State. I was young. Mr. Ruffin told me, "It does not matter that you are close in age to the students. You are the adult, and you are expected to act that way. You are responsible for the children. You have to be responsible for your actions."

Ola R. Luck
Librarian

Mr. Ruffin was a fair man and very respectful. You did not want to do anything to be disrespectful. If he called a person over the loud speaker, he would say, "Come to the office IMMEDIATELY!!!" after calling your name. Everyone would say, "Ooooh!!!! You are in trouble!!!" I got called to the office once. He said, "Geneva Johnson, Victoria Lewis, and Brenda Woolfolk, come to the office IMMEDIATELY!!!" He talked to us about what we had done. Our punishment was to go home and tell our parents. I told him I'd rather work on the chain gang than tell my mother. He said, "No, you have to tell your parents."

Geneva Johnson Thompson
Class of 1963
Business Teacher

ASSISTANT PRINCIPAL

Dr. Walter E. Lowe

I became the assistant principal in 1964. The superintendents were extremely good to me. When I was a teacher, they looked to me to support Mr. Ruffin. The school population grew so large that someone was needed to assist the principal. Superintendent Snead asked me if I wanted to be the assistant principal; I said yes. I assumed the position after it was approved by the school board. I never got any criticisms from the parents. I kept teaching industrial arts for three years. The assistant principal job was more than the superintendent or I had anticipated. Eventually, I stopped teaching.

> Dr. Walter E. Lowe
> Industrial Arts Teacher
> Assistant Principal
> Coach

GUIDANCE COUNSELORS

Marguerite Davis Jackson

I started as an English teacher at Union High in the early 1950s. While teaching at Union High, I also attended New York University, where I received an M.A. in Guidance and Counseling. I also studied at George Washington University. In the 1960s, I became the first guidance counselor at Union High. At first I was a guidance counselor and also taught English. After a while, I became a full-time guidance counselor.

After integration, I continued to work as a guidance counselor at Bowling Green Senior High and later Caroline High when the new school was built, where I worked until I retired.

> Marguerite Davis Jackson
> Class of 1945
> English Teacher
> Guidance Counselor

ASSISTANT PRINCIPAL'S MESSAGE

I am engulfed in mixed emotions as I present this short message to the Class of 1969 . . . .

You are part of an era where the explosion of knowledge is so great that no individual is expected to comprehend all of its complexities but rather to build on a foundation which will allow him to solve problems necessary for self-perpetuation in today's society. Today, the moon, tomorrow—where?

In our society, the number of different jobs . . . has been growing steadily, and the complexity of many of these jobs has grown with the same rapidity. It becomes increasingly apparent that persons with inadequate preparation will be unable to share in the many advantages brought about by this new knowledge.

Today's society presents a challenge which has not been experienced by any other generation . . . I am confident that you possess the aptitudes and abilities to cope with this challenge of today. As you grasp the first rung of the ladder to what is hoped will lead to eventual success, I wish to offer my congratulations to the Class of 1969.

Walter E. Lowe

SOURCE: 1969 UNION HIGH YEARBOOK

My wife, Edith Fraulein Coleman Lowe, graduated from Union High in 1937. She received her teacher's certificate from Virginia State in 1939. She started teaching in the schoolhouses—first Shumansville, then Balty—and taught at Union Elementary after consolidation.

Fraulein Coleman Lowe

She went back to school to obtain a Master's of Education in Counseling and became a guidance counselor at Union High in the 1960s.

> *Dr. Walter E. Lowe*
> *Industrial Arts Teacher*
> *Assistant Principal*
> *Coach*

Teachers

My grandparents were William and Ida Paige. They lived across the street from Union High. Many teachers lived far away: Richmond, Philadelphia, etc. These teachers would stay with them or other people in the neighborhood. They would arrive on Sunday night and go home on Friday evening. Teachers from very far away (eg., Philadelphia) only went home on long breaks or once a month. Some students stayed in the homes, too.

> *Kenneth Paige*
> *Grandson of William and Ida Paige*

The teachers were like an extension of your family. They knew your parents. The minute you did something wrong, they would tell your parents. That would keep you straight.

> *Ivone Parker McReynolds*
> *Class of 1944*

The teachers were very dedicated. They really wanted students to learn. They were well respected in the community. They did all they could to get the students to learn.

I was the valedictorian of my class. Mrs. Virginia Scott Jackson and Mr. Ruffin took me to visit Virginia Union. They talked to my parents about sending me to college. I received a $100 scholarship from Virginia Union and a $75 scholarship from the State Youth Conference. I went to Virginia Union for one year and left to get married.

> *Lillian Richardson Sizer*
> *Class of 1946*

The teachers were great. They became the parents almost. They wanted the students to grow and achieve. It would hurt them when students did not want to learn. They were concerned about the Black students getting an education.

> *Jesse Jackson*
> *Class of 1947*

The teachers were very involved. They explained the importance of education and encouraged the students to go to college.

> *Irene Quash Fields*
> *Class of 1947*

The teachers cared about the students. They made sure you got your work. If you needed help, you could get extra help outside class.

> *Kate Hutchison Samuels*
> *Class of 1950*

The principal and teachers prepared us for life after graduation in many ways. They taught us self respect, that opportunities were out there if you would take advantage of what life had to offer. In life, you must be a part of the solution and not part of the problem. Work hard to get what you want, don't expect it to be given to you. Be a life-long learner.

> *Daisy Jackson Thomas*
> *Class of 1950*

I loved all my teachers. If I had to pick a favorite, I couldn't. They were there for us, and they tried to instill good values in us. They wanted to make sure we got what we needed.

Dorothy Carter Black
Class of 1952

The teachers wanted the best for the students. They wanted the students to work to the best of our ability. They tried to prepare us for life after high school. Mr. Ruffin and the teachers were involved with the parents. If they could not get a student's cooperation, the ultimate threat was to talk to [the student's] parents.

Vivian Garnett Coleman
Class of 1953

The teachers were very good. They tried to instill in us to be the best. They would tell us because we were Black we had to be better than the others. They encouraged us to work to our highest potential and build a solid foundation.

Evelyn Wright Thompson
Class of 1958

The teachers did a good job. They were a wonderful group of teachers. They would take students aside who seemed upset to talk to the student to see what was wrong. They were concerned; they were like our parents away from home.

Beulah Collins
Class of 1959

I enjoyed school and learned a lot from the teachers; not just academics but morals. Mrs. Banks would always talk to us about being young ladies.

The teachers cared about the total student. School was like a family. The teachers did not make a lot of money. They were not teaching for the money; they tried their best to give the students all they could. The teachers knew how to take a little and make a lot.

The students were required to purchase their textbooks. The teachers had text books they would loan students whose parents could not afford to buy books. The students would return the book at the end of the year.

Barbara Jones Rock
Class of 1961

The teachers really cared about the students. They would talk to them and encourage them. Mrs. Wilson [music teacher] would not allow students to say they could not do something. Ms. Ruth Brown [physical education teacher] would often tell students, "You can do anything if you put your mind to."

Aterita Baker Brown
Attended Union High from 1958 to 1961

The teachers were very qualified and really cared about students. They would talk to the students about life.

Thomas Davis
Class of 1964

We looked up to the teachers. They were our role models. They had nice homes and cars. They made sure we got our lessons. If a student asked a question, they would take the time and explain. They were always willing to help.

Waverly Minor
Class of 1962

The teachers knew you by name and were very supportive. They knew about you and knew your parents. They shared their wisdom with us. They would often say, "I've been where you are going." They really cared about us, and the students listened to them. I admired the teachers. They were always dressed so nice; the women wore heels and dresses, no pants. The men wore suits and ties. The teachers would stand out because of the way they dressed. The guidance counselors helped us prepare for college. They made sure we filled out the applications and took the college entrance exams. We had to rely on the teachers and guidance counselors for direction. We visited Virginia State on high school day. Our school had a bus that took us there. We took a tour of the campus, went to a football game, and ate in the dining hall with the college students. I knew that was the school I wanted to go to. I applied only to Virginia State, and I was accepted.

Florence Lee Rhue
Class of 1965

Most of the teachers were very capable and had the students' interests at heart. They pushed students to do well.

Patricia Sizer Adams
Class of 1964

The teachers were very professional. They were well groomed and spoke very well. They were interested in the students' learning. They were firm but cared about us. The students were very orderly. They respected the teachers, and the teachers respected the students.

Sherrillyn LaVerne Smith Silver
Class of 1965

The teachers were very giving of themselves. They acted as counselors, parents, and advisors. They would feed you if you were hungry and help you with your personal problems. They cared about the whole person, with building knowledge and character. They were role models in the way the dressed, carried themselves, and spoke. They showed students how to act through their actions. The teachers had a way of making you want learn. You were going to get it, one way or another.

William Brawner
Class of 1966

The teachers did not just teach subjects. They also gave us life lessons. They talked to us about getting along in the world and how to deal with racism. They would always tell us, "Being good is not good enough. You have to be great at whatever you do." They encouraged us to strive for perfection. We were told we had to be twice as good as the next person. These lessons pre-

pared us for life and allowed us to be successful in a segregated world. Lessons taught at home were reinforced at school.

Williabel Jones Davis
Class of 1966

The teachers were sincerely interested in students and were committed to education. They worked with students in and out of class to make sure they learned. They would inform parents if there was a problem. The teachers took pride in teaching, exhibited a strong commitment to their subject matter, and cared about you as a student and person. They took pride in their role in helping the students to contribute positively to society.

Carolyn Garnett Epps
Class of 1966

The teachers were held in high esteem. They were concerned with what was good for the students and good for the school. They wanted students to grow up and be successful. They would talk to us about morals, being a good citizen, and being civic minded.

Arthur Sizer Jr.
Attended Union High 1967–1969
Graduated from Ladysmith in 1972

Teachers encouraged us to work hard and take our studies seriously. Most set high expectations. We all knew we were going to college, but we did not know how. When we were in college, the teachers would come to homecoming. They would give us money when they saw us on campus.

Geneva Johnson Thompson
Class of 1963
Business Teacher

The teachers really knew the students, cared about them, and were concerned. They had the support of the parents and the community. Most teachers lived and went to church in the area; therefore, they knew your parents.

Students did well because the teachers had very high standards. The teachers would not accept a student not trying. They instilled a sense of pride in the students and stressed the value of education. There was a strong emphasis on academics and going to college. Parents and people in the community had the same expectations.

If a student had difficulty with a lesson, the teacher would work with the student until they understood. There was study hall where you get extra help from student tutors.

Students were very disciplined. They respected adults and did what they were told. The teachers were the students' friends in the sense that they would help you. However, they were not your pal. It was clear that the teachers were in charge of the school. My parents told me, if I had a problem with the teacher I should tell them, and they would talk to the teacher.

Calvin Taylor
Class of 1969

I feel that we were some of the most blessed children who attended Union High School. We had teachers who were interested in our physical, mental, and religious learning. We received one-on-one learning, as well, as love.

Judith Jones Budd
Class of 1953

Union High and Elementary Faculty 1930–1931, (l. to r.) first row: Rev. Andrew P. Young, A. McKee Banks, Annie Fortune, Mattie G. Fields; second row: Virginia Scott Jackson, Hovey Rice Young (principal), Naomi Miller.
COURTESY THE ARCHIE G. RICHARDSON PAPERS, ACCESSION #1997-77, SPECIAL COLLECTIONS AND ARCHIVES, JOHNSTON MEMORIAL LIBRARY, VIRGINIA STATE UNIVERSITY, PETERSBURG, VIRGINIA.

Elementary and high school teachers, (l. to r.) front row: Annie Fortune Baylor, Pauline Shelton, George Ruffin (principal), Elizabeth Holden, Lavinia Anderson Guss; second row: Mary Banks, Muriel Washington Bennett, Sudie Perry, Elizabeth Gwathmey; third row: Mary Ellen White, Dr. Walter E. Lowe, Virginia Scott Jackson, J. Shelby Guss; fourth row: Reginald A. Beverly, Alma Upton, A. McKee Banks, James Luckie.
SOURCE: 1949 UNION HIGH YEARBOOK.

(l. to r.) Virginia Scott Jackson, Elizabeth Moody, A. McKee Banks, Louise B. Carter, Andrew P. Young, Mary Banks, Hovey R. Young (principal), circa late 1930s.
COURTESY WESLEY T. CARTER.

(l. to r.) Front row: Andrew P. Young, Louise B. Carter, Hovey R. Young (principal), Elizabeth Moody, Commodore N. Bennett; back row: George Ruffin, Mary Banks, A. McKee Banks, Virginia Scott Jackson, circa late 1930s– early 1940s. COURTESY WESLEY T. CARTER.

Elementary and high school teachers. (l. to r.) Front row: Celestine Ragland, Marguerite Davis, Sallie Pankey, Frauline Lowe, Annie Fortune Baylor, unknown, unknown, unknown; second row: George Ruffin (principal), Ruth Wilson, Elizabeth Holden, Elizabeth Gwathmey, Bessie Johnson Beverly, Sudie Perry, Alma Upton, Mary Banks; third row: James Luckie, Edward Barksdale, J. Shelby Guss, Mary E. White, Reginald Beverly, Dr. Walter Lowe, Christopher Lee. back row: Lloyd Boxley, A. McKee Banks, unknown, unknown.
SOURCE: *1952 UNION HIGH YEARBOOK.*

A. MCKEE BANKS— AGRICULTURAL

A. McKee Banks

My godfather, who I affectionately called Uncle Mack, was a mentor and compassionate teacher to generations of students. He had a great rapport with them—a mutual respect—always encouraging them to do their personal best. He stressed the importance of pursuing an education—the key to endless opportunities. Additionally, he would drive students to and from school and give them money for school lunch.

Diane Boxley Burnett
Daughter of Lloyd L. Boxley (teacher)

I was a student of both late Mr. L. L. Boxley and Mr. McKee Banks during the years 1958 to 1962. As I recall, they both taught us life skills, as well as class subject matter. They each would often teach us how to be gentlemen to ladies, as well as good manners and proper etiquette. We would often do role-playing in our classes, wherein they each would critique our performance. Many times, we were embarrassed, but they would use it as a teaching moment rather than ridicule us.

Additionally, they each were available for one-on-one personal talks about anything to help us.

James M. Johnson
Class of 1962

Mr. Banks offered to pay the entire cost of college education for four years for me if I did good in school. For that reason, I will always remember him.

Marshall Washington
Class of 1969

MARY B. BANKS— HOME ECONOMICS

Mary B. Banks

Mary Black Banks received her undergraduate degree in home economics from Virginia State College in Petersburg, Virginia, in 1938. She joined the Union High staff in the late 1930s as a home economics teacher. In August 1945, she left her teaching position to become a state supervisor of home economics education for the Virginia Department of Education, a position she held until 1947.

She resumed her home economics teaching position at Union High in 1947. In addition to teaching, she also served as the advisor for New Homemakers of America and Future Homemakers of America, J. R. Thomas Camp, Home Economics Education in Virginia, and the Caroline County Cannery. Banks obtained an M.S. degree from Cornell University in 1950. After integration in 1969, she continued to teach home economics at Bowling Green Senior High School and retired in 1971 after 40 years of teaching.

Mary Banks was very active in several organizations. She was a strong supporter of her alma mater, Virginia State College-Virginia State University, and often encouraged students to attend the university. After his death, she established the A. McKee Banks Virginia State University Scholarship Fund in honor of her husband, a Union High agricultural teacher.

In her later years, Banks was honored by many organizations for her contribution to the community, various civics organizations, and her alma mater. During one of these occasions, she mentioned that one of her pleasures was meeting former students who say they have benefited from her instruction and counseling.[41]

INFORMATION OBTAINED FROM VARIOUS NEWS ARTICLES.

PUT HIM HIGH ON THE LIST OF THOSE WHO COUNT
TRIBUTE TO MR. BANKS

In his 37 years as agriculture teacher at Union High School, he elevated vocational training in agriculture to a top position in Caroline County and in the state of Virginia. Put him high on the list of men who really count, for he taught his boys to believe in the marvels of the products of the soil and in the fascination of animal husbandry. Think about it! He has seen almost twenty of the young men whose lives he touched receive their B.S. degrees in agriculture. Eight of them were teachers in Virginia, all at the same time!!! Think of it! He has even seen some of them get their master's degrees in phases of agriculture. He has had the courage to present to the youth of the county the absolute principles of living learned only through his experience and knowledge. This is attested to by the number of "hi-ya, Mr. Banks" cards that he receives from as far away as Pakistan, where a former student is administering a government farm program.

Put him high on the list of the men who really count because he thinks about people a great deal, not just once in a while. This is revealed in his loyalty and devotion to his Alma Mater (Virginia State), his fraternity (Omega Psi Phi), his church (St. John), and his Masonic Lodge (F&AM Masons-Welcome 125). Ask any of his students who attend or who have attended Virginia State to whom have they turned when they needed financial assistance or a little-stay-in school push? Right away they will answer, "Mr. Banks, of course."

Think about him, about how he is always willing to contribute or go to the bat for a worthy professional, civic, religious, or fraternal cause.

Thank you, Mr. Banks, Thanks a lot. We shall always keep you HIGH ON THE LIST OF MEN WHO REALLY COUNT.

Mary White Dungee

SOURCE: THE POINTER REVIEW, JUNE 1967

Mrs. Mary Banks was my favorite teacher, and she taught me home economics. She took me to her home on many weekends to stay with her and her husband, McKee Banks. They did not have any children of their own, but they treated me like their own. I learned how to cook and sew in her class. My mother VeEtta Rebecca Burruss Twiggs (she was one of 18 children born to Thomas Burruss and Ida Woolfolk Burruss) graduated from Union High in 1927. She taught school after going to Virginia State College. (My mother VeEtta was the only child of the 18 who received a college degree.) She never taught me to cook. Whenever I asked her to let me cook, she said "Go up stairs to your room and study your lesson." Mr. and Mrs. Banks took me to see my first live play on stage at age 14. I was happy and so excited.

When I got married, I took my husband and three sons to plays. Until this day, I still love going to plays, dinner theaters, concerts, and movies, which Mrs. Banks introduced me to as a teenager. I also love traveling. I belong to four traveling clubs. I try to take a trip if no more than a one-day trip every month. Mrs. Pauline Boxley, who is my dear friend and teacher at Union High, knew how much I loved Mrs. Banks. When she passed, Mrs. Boxley asked me to write and read a poem at her funeral. She passed Jan. 9, 2005. I was very happy to do so. I always said when I grow up, I wanted to be just like Mrs. Banks. She had such a beautiful strut. I thought everything about her was beautiful. She was good looking, had a good shape, and I loved her so much. She spoke perfect English so eloquently. All teachers had tough love for us but were caring, loving, and strict disciplinarians.

Bert Twiggs Nichols
Class of 1948

Mrs. Banks was a Virginia State alumna. She encouraged students to attend her school. I went to Virginia State. I stayed with one of her friends for two years. It helped me save money for school.

Vivian Garnett Coleman
Class of 1953

In addition to teaching home economics Mrs. Banks would always talk to us about being a lady. She would tell us not to wear tight skirts. She said you should be able to catch your skirt in the hip area, pull it up, and let it fall freely down. It if got stuck, that meant your skirt was too tight. She would tell us to always be a lady. To cross your legs at the ankle when you sit down and keep your legs closed.

Sherrillyn LaVerne Smith Silver
Class of 1965

Mrs. Banks made our lives so good. She taught us to improvise and make do with what we had. She was such an asset to us. She taught us how to act like ladies. She would say, "Don't hang on the corner and talk to people across the street." "Don't walk around with cigarettes hanging out your mouth." She taught us how to dress, wear makeup, and balance a checkbook.

She came to my community to organize a sewing club at Sycamore school. She would come twice a month. She would stop by and pick up my mother. The women would go to the school house for the sewing club.

Ivone Parker McReynolds
Class of 1944

Mrs. Banks was very caring and nurturing. She always stressed being a lady. She would say, "Ladies do not chew gum in public." She would talk to us about hygiene, the importance of being clean and wearing clean clothes. She would monitor the girl's bathroom and make sure no one was smoking or skipping class. She would stand in the hallway when classes were changing to monitor students' behavior. If she saw someone acting inappropriately, she would pull them into her classroom and talk to them.

Catherine Ferguson
Class of 1969

A TRIBUTE TO MRS. BANKS

We, the friends and graduates of Union High School have many things in common. We shared a school, a community, some of the same friends, and a lot of the same memories. These memories, good, bad, or indifferent are our own and are remembered by each of us in a unique way.

Tonight, I'd like us all to search our memories. I know that if may be a little hard for some of us to think back that far, but let us try to recall our eighth-grade year. I'd like you to focus on one teacher, a lady that each of us probably had an encounter with. I'm willing to bet that most of us have the same lady in mind.

Ladies, I know you remember how scared we were. I know you remember bobby socks and gym and how loud we were. Trying to be seen by that good-looking senior that just walked by with Carmen Moore on his arm.

Guys, can't you just remember how you envisioned being on the basketball team but finding out that guys like Emory and Billy Bird, Big O and Calvin Miner and Cadillac had it all sewed up.

OK, I think I've got the old wheels turning. You do remember that year!

That year, there was a lady reminding us the we're now high school students and expected to behave like young men and young women. This lady was there giving advice that we really didn't want to hear, but we listened.

Now, think about your junior year. That lady is still there teaching and advising us girls to act like young ladies because young men don't respect girls that don't respect themselves. I know you remember. This lady would gently take us aside and say, "Now, Miss, don't you think that skirt is a wee bit too short or a just wee bit too tight?" All the girls know her method for demonstrating this point!

Don't you guys laugh. She would just as quickly pull you aside and say, "Now, you are a really nice-looking fellow, and your parents work hard to keep you in clean clothes so you will look nice in school. Now, why didn't you use deodorant this morning?"

This lady was unique. She was concerned for all of us, all of the time. She had our good in mind, and it showed, not just in her words but also in her actions.

You know we all had a sort of love-hate relationship with her. We hated to be singled out by her. We hated it when she reinforced the values and morals our parents tried to instill in us. But we loved it when she complimented us and looked at us—we are beautiful people, and we can be proud of the way we've turned out partly because of her concern, because of her love for us.

We, the students of Union High School, all have some of the same memories of this lady. Just because this lady played such an important part in our sneak preview into adulthood. Just because we love her for all that she did, we'd like to honor her tonight:

Ladies and Gentlemen, on behalf of the entire student body of the CLASS of 1965, I give you MRS. MARY BANKS.

Written by:
Eleanor Thomas Brown
Class of 1965

SPEECH GIVEN AT CLASS OF 1965 20TH REUNION TO INTRODUCE MARY BANKS. COURTESY ELEANOR THOMAS HAWKINS.

Start Here

Mrs. Banks was a very caring person. She would observe the students and knew what was going on in the family. She would reach out to help you any way she could. My mother wanted me to go to college. I was having trouble getting help. I told Mrs. Banks that I wanted to go to college and needed some help. She said, "Let me see what I can do." She helped me get two scholarships to Virginia State. One was from the Virginia State Alumni Association; the other was from the NAACP.

Joyce Woolfolk Spencer
Attended Union High 1967–1969
Graduated from Bowling Green
Senior High School 1971

Mrs. Banks was my favorite teacher. She really had a vested interest in all her students. She did not care what side of the tracks you were from—she treated everyone the same. She would give us advice and lecture us. She would never correct someone in front of everyone. She would pull you aside and talk to you. Mini skirts had just come out, and she would talk to us about not wearing our skirts too short or too tight.

I was very shy. One day she had me stand in front of the class. I was dreading it when she called my name because I was expecting her to say this is how you should not dress. Instead she said, "This is the way I want my ladies to dress. This is an appropriate length dress and fit." She had me

---

TRIBUTE TO MRS. MARY BLACK BANKS '28, '36

EVELYN P. RAGLAND, SECRETARY CAROLINE COUNTY CHAPTER VSU ALUMNI ASSOCIATION

"For thou has been shelter for me and a strong tower from the enemy.
I will abide in thy tabernacle forever. I will trust in the covert of the wings"
Psalm 61, Verses 3 and 4

The Lord was Mrs. Banks's shelter. She was like a mother to me. I've known her all my life. When I think about her and my life, I remember the days when I was "yea high" when she gave me my first red and white sweater to symbolize Delta Sigma Theta Sorority. She was also a religious person maintaining active membership at Shiloh Baptist Church, Bowling Green, Virginia. Mrs. Banks was truly a community person who touched many. She was active in the NAACP, was a Home Economics instructor in Caroline County for many years, served as president of the Richmond Virginia Chapter Delta Sigma Theta Sorority, active in the Petersburg Alumnae Chapter Delta Sigma Theta Sorority, served as president for our Caroline County Chapter of the Virginia State University Alumni Association, and served as Worthy Matron Welcome Chapter #129, Order of the Eastern Star.

In the Caroline County Chapter Virginia State University Alumni Association, we give scholarships to students attending Virginia State University. Mrs. Banks was a strong sponsor of the scholarship honoring her late husband, Mr. A. McKee Banks.

Mrs. Banks was like a mother because she taught me cooking at school and often gave motherly advice. I remember the days when she and my mother, the late Mrs. Celestine C. Ragland, would work tirelessly in our Community Cannery. She was my sister in two ways. I remember the days of NHA (New Homemakers of America) and FHA (Future Homemakers of America) when students would visit the summer camp (J. R. Thomas Camp) and go to the state fair in the fall.

I will surely miss her. We will all miss her. She lived a good life. Let us think about the good times we had with her. She has left her temporary shelter of 95 years and is now in a better place to rejoin (after over 28 years), her late husband, Mr. A. McKee Banks, other close friends, and associates.
We shall all miss her smiling face and kind heart. Let us bid farewell. The Caroline County Chapter Virginia State University Alumni Association desires you think of her and of a deserving student and donate funds to the A. M. Banks Scholarship Fund in her memory.

SOURCE: VIRGINIA STATE UNIVERSITY ALUMNI MAGAZINE, VOLUME 5(1)

pull up my skirt and let it fall down to demonstrate that it was not too tight. It gave me such a lift to have the teacher point me out as someone who did something appropriate, especially since I was a poor kid from the wrong side of the tracks. It made me want to work harder to please her.

Eleanor Thomas Hawkins
Class of 1965

Mrs. Mary Banks and Mrs. Celestine Ragland taught me Home Economics. In addition to cooking and sewing, they taught the social graces: how to walk, sit, stand, and wear the appropriate attire for the right occasion—in a word, to be a lady. When a student completed their class, it was like having gone to a high-class finishing school or a charm school. We had to walk with a book on our heads. We were told "a lady crosses her legs at the ankle, not the knee." "Do not chew gum in class, church," etc. A tight skirt should not be too tight. "If you lift it and let it go, it should fall by itself. If you lift it, and it stays up, it's too tight."

Williabel Jones Davis
Class of 1966

COMMODORE N. (C.N.) BENNETT– HISTORY

Mr. C. N. Bennett taught me at Sycamore [elementary school]. He would get materials from workshops outside the county and bring it back to teach the students. He would have pictures, books, and so on about Black history. He was determined to give the students a good foundation. I will never forget him.

He also taught me history in high school. The English and history teachers would help students participate in the Oratory Contest. Mr. Luckie was the math teacher. He wrote my speech. I went to a competition at Armstrong and won. Mrs. V. S. Jackson and Mr. Ruffin took me. It was so nice to see the pleasure on their faces when I won.

Ivone Parker McReynolds
Class of 1944

REGINALD A. BEVERLY–MATHEMATICS

Reginald A. Beverly

I graduated from Union High in 1933; there were 13 people in my class. I went to Virginia State College (now Virginia State University), where I majored in science and minored in math. I graduated in 1938 and taught for two years at Louisa Training School in Louisa County, Virginia.

I came to Union High in 1940. I taught all subjects except French; my language was German. I mainly taught math, science, and sometimes English. In the 1940s, I was paid $85 per month. I also drove the school bus for 20 years for Union High. The county owned the bus. I drove it to school, taught school, and drove the bus after school.

I was drafted in 1941. I received a letter about one month before I had to report for duty. I went to school on December 5th 1941, called the roll, and then went to Bowling Green, where I caught the bus to Richmond, Virginia. I had to report for duty at Fort Meade for basic training. After basic training, I was sent to Fort Belvoir to attend surveyor school. The military needed surveyors, but they did not have time to teach them math. Since I was a math teacher, they sent me to surveyor school. I was a regimental surveyor for the 95th Engineer Regiment. We built 300 miles of the Alcan Highway (sometimes called the Alaskan Highway). It went from Dawson Creek, British Columbia, through the Yukon Territory to Alaska. I was discharged on September 15, 1945. The superintendent told me to take a week vacation and then report to work. I started teaching again in September. Mr. Luckie came to teach when I was drafted. He continued to teach when I returned because they needed more math teachers.

My time at Union High was a pleasant experience. I wanted my students to master all of their subjects and participate with other schools in the math and science competitions. One year, I took students to a math competition at Hoffman-Boston High School in Alexandria, Virginia. Phillip Byrd won 1st place in the math competition, and three brothers—Woodrow Wilson James, Calvin Coolidge James, and Theodore Roosevelt James—won 1st, 2nd, and 3rd place in the trigonometry competition (I don't remember which one won which place.) We were very surprised that we won because Union High was a small school compared to the other schools in the competition (Manassas Regional High School, Hoffman-Boston, and Walker Grant).

While teaching, I worked at the North Anna Power Station during the summer. In 1968, they offered me job as a mathematician to keep up with cubic yards of earth work for dams and dikes. (This is how the construction companies were paid). I was released from my contract with the Caroline School Board and went to work there.

Reginald A. Beverly
Class of 1933
Mathematics Teacher

Mr. Beverly was so smart. He was the nicest teacher. Sometimes I thought he was too nice because some students would act up. He wouldn't yell at them. He was a good teacher.

Florence Lee Rhue
Class of 1965

Mr. Beverly was a nice, kind, gentle person. He would work with students; he wanted them to succeed.

Gladys Fitzhugh-Pemberton
Class of 1964

LLOYD BOXLEY–AGRICULTURAL

Lloyd L. Boxley

Lloyd Boxley was a 1938 graduate of Union High School. After graduation he worked as a construction worker helping build Caroline High School. In 1939, he entered Virginia State College (now Virginia State University) and majored in agriculture. He left college in 1942 when he was drafted into the Army, where he served as a Supply NCO and attained the rank of technical sergeant before his honorable discharge in 1945. After his military service, he returned to Virginia State College and graduated in 1947 with a B.S. degree in agriculture.

After graduating, he returned to Caroline County, where he taught agricultural night classes to veterans and joined the Union High faculty as an agriculture teacher. He also served as an advisor for the New Farmers of America and Future Farmers of America and taught adult farm machinery classes at night. After integration, he taught agriculture at Bowling Green Senior High School and Caroline High School. In addition to teaching, he also managed the Caroline Community Cannery for many years and continued this service after his retirement. After his death in 2005, the Cannery was renamed the Lloyd L. Boxley Cannery in his honor.

Boxley retired from teaching in 1984 after 37 years of teaching. When asked to reflect on his teaching experience, he said, "I like to see students get an education, to strive to get good jobs. I have worked with them, and they've put it to use in life." He also stated he tried to help students become good citizens and it made him feel good when he saw his students become independent and successful in their own lives.[42]

FROM INTERVIEW WITH PAULINE SHELTON BOXLEY (WIFE) AND VARIOUS NEWS ARTICLES

Mr. Lloyd Boxley Sr. had a major influence on my life during my last two years at Ruther Glen Elementary and my years at Union High School. When I was in the sixth grade, Mr. Boxley inducted our family farm tractor into the Vocational Agriculture Repair Shop at Union High School for a self-help engine overhaul project. This project was a big deal for my father Douglas "Peck" Woolfolk because he only had to pay for the parts and materials used to overhaul the engine. The labor was free because my family was able to provide the labor pool (consisting of me, my father, and my brother Charlie, who was five years older than me).

We were required to disassemble the tractor and the engine, clean the useable parts, install the replacement parts, and reassemble the engine and the tractor, all under the technical stewardship of Mr. Boxley and a local agri-mechanical engineer, Mr. Michael Wright Sr. This overhaul project was indeed a big deal for me, too, because Mr. Boxley allowed me (an eager 11-year-old) to work in the Agricultural Repair Shop even though I was not in high school yet and not eligible to be a member of the New Farmers of America (NFA).

So, when I entered Union High School in 1963, after graduating from the two-room Ruther Glen Elementary, I signed up for vocational agriculture with Mr. Boxley as my instructor. He continued to provide coaching and stewardship that guided me into top leadership roles at the local chapters of NFA and FFA (Future Farmers of America) and lead me to enter Virginia State University in 1967. My life has been more than expected because Mr. Boxley was my coach. My sincere thanks!

Rogers Woolfolk, LTC (Ret), U.S. Army
Class of 1967

My Dad was a devoted teacher and mentor to generations of students. Over the years, his former students have shared uplifting stories with my family, expressing the positive impact Dad had on their lives. To know him was to know his wisdom, support, patience, and strength. He would reflect on his own personal life experiences while helping his students to confront and understand their own daily trials, as well as acknowledge their accomplishments. But he always reminded them to look forward and embrace opportunities, always offering his guidance, advice, and help. Dad exhibited this same passion and enthusiasm for excellence with me and my brother, Lloyd Jr. We were blessed to have him in our lives.

Diane Boxley Burnett
Daughter

Mr. Boxley was like family and a very important person in my life. He was as close to me as my own relatives. What I learned from him helped me as I became a grown man. He gave me good advice in many ways. He taught me how to raise and care for hogs, how to prepare and cut up the meat. He showed me how to use the equipment in the Community Cannery to make sausage, to render and can lard, to clean the equipment properly and put everything back in place for others. He gave me good advice for life.

Marshall Washington
Class of 1969

I took the agriculture class during the second semester of my freshman year. Enrolling in this class was the best thing that has ever happened to me! It was the year that I met Mr. Lloyd L. Boxley.

Mr. Boxley was a unique person. Other than my father, there had been only one other male individual that had influenced my life, and that was Mr. Boxley. It appeared that Mr. Boxley made it a priority to get to know his students. Each day was an amazing new adventure. We had fun doing whatever he had planned for us, yet we learned so much. It was one of those classes you looked forwarded to attending. Not only did we learn about the principles of agriculture, we also learned principles of leadership that one could use in everyday life.

Mr. Boxley influenced me to become involved in public speaking. This experience led to a meeting with the head of the agricultural department at Virginia State College, where I delivered a speech entitled, "Opportunities in Agriculture." I will never forget this speech. The introduction began as follows:

"The Lord God spoke to the serpent, He spoke to the woman, and then to Adam He said in part: 'Cursed is the ground because of you. You shall eat of the fruit of the grounds.' Thus began agriculture in the land, and thus began man's plight to toil, and opportunities have abounded ever since."

Because of Mr. Boxley's role and influence in my life as a youth, I enrolled in college and received a degree in agriculture.

Stanley O. Jones
Class of 1963

Mr. Boxley was a great teacher. I learned a welding trade under him. At that point and time of my life I didn't think that it would help me, but it has. When I owned my own dump truck business and started farming, I purchased my own welding machine and was able to use the techniques that I learned in shop under Mr. Boxley. Mr. Boxley also taught me agriculture, and as of today I am a farmer. We even learned how to repair small engines.

Bernard Freeman
Class of 1967

PAULINE SHELTON BOXLEY– HOME ECONOMICS (SUBSTITUTE)

After graduating from Buckingham County High School in 1943, I relocated to New Jersey and worked for the federal government. I made condensers for radios for the military during World War II. My goal was to work a year, attend a college there, and become a nurse. It was instilled in

Pauline Shelton Boxley

me to go to Virginia State College (now Virginia State University), major in home economics, and become a teacher. After working one year, I did go to Virginia State College. I continued working in New Jersey during the summers while I was in school at Virginia State.

After graduating from Virginia State in 1948 with a degree in home economics, I was offered a teaching position at Union High School because the regular teacher, Mrs. Celestine Ragland, was going out on maternity leave. After teaching during the 1948–1949 school year, my plan was to return to New Jersey and fulfill my goals there. However, the superintendent, Mr. W. A. Vaughan said, "You don't need to leave the county because Mrs. Ragland is returning. I can offer you a job in the elementary grades." He gave me two weeks to

decide on one of three schools. Finally, I stayed to teach grades four through seven at St. James Elementary School in the St. James Community. Immediately, I began taking courses at Virginia State College, the University of Virginia, and received a master's degree and became certified to elementary education.

I was asked by Mr. Ruffin the principal to teach home economics again during the 1954–1955 and 1956–1957 school years during the leave of absence of the same teacher. The home economics curriculum consisted of cooking, sewing, consumer education, and money management. The New Homemakers of America Club was also a part of the home economics program. This organization offered students the opportunity to become members of the local, state, and national programs. They also took part in fashion shows, talent shows, fixed boxes of goods for the needy, and decorated floats for the May Day Parade. The home economics schoolwork was a carried over as home projects: doing family sewing, helping to plan and serve the family meals, and being a good homemaker.

At Union High School, students were taught to work twice as hard to get an education, to get a job, and to be prepared to compete with students who had all the advantages in everything. They needed to know and were taught how to interact with others, have social graces, and how to present themselves to others. Union High School was a place of learning that gave students a good foundation to be successful in life.

I will always remember my years at Union High. I established a great relationship not only with Mrs. Ragland and Mrs. Banks but also with the students, the faculty, parents, and the communities. Teaching in the Caroline County School System as an educator until 1995 was an unforgettable experience. I would not have changed for anybody, including the plans I had made previously for New Jersey.

Pauline Shelton Boxley
Substitute Home Economics Teacher

I was a student of Miss Pauline Shelton (now Mrs. Pauline Boxley) during the year 1948–1949. She taught me how to use the sewing machine and how to place a pattern on the material. I helped to make dresses for the May Day floats. It was a joy to be in her class.

Vivian Garnett Coleman
Class of 1953

LOUISE BYRD CARTER– ENGLISH AND FRENCH

Louise Byrd Carter

Louise Byrd Carter graduated from Caroline County Training School in 1929 and was the class valedictorian. She attended Virginia Union University and graduated 1935. That same year, she became a teacher at Union High and taught there for seven years. Originally, she taught elementary grades and later high school English and French and served as the choir director. During this time she developed, with the support of elementary teachers, the first County Music Festival, which involved all the county children, including the high school chorus. The festival became a very successful and popular event and was considered a training affair for all of the participants.

FROM AN INTERVIEW WITH CARTER'S HUSBAND, WESLEY T. CARTER, AND NOTES WRITTEN BY LOUIS B. CARTER IN 1999

I took music lessons from Mrs. Louise Byrd Carter when I was about 10 years old. My mother paid Mrs. Carter 50 cents per lesson. There was a piano in chapel at Union High. We would go there and play the piano. Mrs. Carter taught me enough so I could play the pump organ at church [Second Mt. Calvary in New Baltimore]. The first songs I learned to play were the hymns "Just As I Am" and "My Faith Looks Up to Thee."

I started playing the pump organ at church at age 10 and continued to play when I went away to Virginia Union College. I was paid 50 cents. My freshman year in college, I would catch the Trailways bus from Virginia Union to Bowling Green, Virginia, in order to play the pump organ in church.

Mrs. Lucy Monte cooked meals for the dormitory at Union High. She was also in charge of the choir at Second Mount Calvary. She would tell me the hymns for next Sunday, and I would practice with Mrs. Carter.

Marguerite Davis Jackson
Class of 1945
English Teacher
Guidance Counselor

MARY WHITE DUNGEE– HISTORY, ENGLISH, GOVERNMENT

Mary White Dungee

I was very shy. Mrs. Dungee wanted to help me to get over my shyness. She would give me money and send me to the cafeteria to buy her lunch. She would tell the other students not to buy it for me because she wanted me to learn not to be shy. Eventually I got over my shyness.

Kate Hutcheson Samuels
Class of 1950

Mrs. Dungee was very knowledgeable. She made you like geography and could tell us things about other parts of the world. Because of her, I know about countries, and so on, today.

Florence Rhue
Class of 1965

My son [Michael McReynolds] owns a law firm. Mrs. Dungee was very instrumental in pushing him. The teachers pushed the students; they did not slack up on them.

Ivone Parker McReynolds
Class of 1944

Mrs. Dungee was my government teacher. She is one of the reasons I voted the first time I was old enough, and I have never missed an opportunity to vote in an election whether it is a presidential election or a local election. In those days, you had to be 21 to vote. She is also responsible for the type of bedroom furniture I have in my master bedroom. She invited the valedictorian and me to spend the night at her home one evening. With parental consent, Sandra and I enjoyed an overnight at Mrs. Dungee's home. She had a king-size, four-post, tobacco-leaf bed. That evening I decided that I would have that type of bed in my home someday. When at age 27 my husband and I built our first home, we furnished our master bedroom with a king-size bed. Today my master suite sports a four-post, tobacco-leaf, king-size bed with matching Victorian dresser, chest of drawers, and nightstand.

Williabel Jones Davis
Class of 1966

J. SHELBY GUSS– GOVERNMENT

James Shelby Guss graduated from Union High School in 1940 and attended Virginia Union University. The draft interrupted his college education, and he served with distinction in the Pacific Theater with the Army Air Corps. At the end of the war, he re-

J. Shelby Guss

turned to Virginia Union and used the GI Bill to continue his education. He graduated in 1948 with a bachelor's degree in education.

He returned to Caroline County and taught history and government at Union High. While teaching at Union High, he wrote the words for the school's Alma Mater. Always seeking ways to improve his teaching skills, Guss attended George Washington University during the summer in the mid-1950s and obtained a master's degree in 1958.

In 1959, he became principal of Union Elementary School. In 1964, he was elected president of the Virginia Teacher's Association. During his tenure, he thought of many creative and innovative ways to improve the organization such as leading a work study group to 11 European countries, traveling to Washington, D.C., to support a bill strengthening education, as well as visiting the White House at the invitation of President Lyndon Johnson.

During integration he worked very hard to ensure the transition was smooth. As principal of the Bowling Green Elementary School (formerly Union High Elementary School), he worked to bring people together. He helped merge the all-Black Virginia Teachers' Association with the all-White Virginia Education Association and worked diligently to ensure the new organization improved the quality of education for all students in Virginia.

In 1970, Guss resigned as principal of Bowling Green Elementary School to become a field director for the Virginia Education Association, where his launched a variety of innovative programs to better serve teachers. Active in several educational and political organizations in Caroline County and Virginia, Guss was known as a dedicated, conciliatory leader for positive and constructive change, as well as a tireless advocate for education and public service.

FROM VARIOUS NEWS ARTICLES AND A NARRATIVE FOR A 1999 SLIDE SHOW HONORING GUSS

Mr. Shelby Guss was my government teacher. He was a great advisor and friend. You could always go to him to get help you needed about anything.

Rev. Joseph Dobbins
Class of 1959

MILDRED EASTER HARRIS– COMMERCE AND BUSINESS EDUCATION

Mildred Easter White

My favorite teacher was Miss Mildred Easter. She had high expectations for her students and truly wanted them to excel. She pushed her students to do their best; she did not allow them to say "I can't do . . . ." I admired the way she carried herself. She always dressed professionally. I became a business teacher because of her. After I graduated from Virginia State College, I became a business teacher at Roosevelt High School in Washington, D.C. I taught there for 37 years.

> *Gladys Fitzhugh-Pemberton*
> *Class of 1964*

MARGUERITE DAVIS JACKSON– ENGLISH

Marguerite Davis Jackson

I graduated from Union High in 1945 and attended Virginia Union. After graduation from Virginia Union, I taught primary grades for one year at Union in the USO building. Ms. T. T. Jackson, an English teacher at Union High, was from Richmond, Virginia. In the early 1950s, she accepted a position at Virginia Union at the beginning of the second semester, and I was reassigned to teach English at Union High. I also taught 8th grade science and civics. I became a guidance counselor in the 1960s.

My years at Union High were a rewarding time. The students had a strong desire to learn. The parents were very interested in their children and excited about their children learning. They were also very cooperative, loving, and caring. I am grateful for the precious memories of Union High that I share with my family and friends.

> *Marguerite Davis Jackson*
> *Class of 1945*
> *English Teacher*
> *Guidance Counselor*

HAD IT NOT BEEN FOR YOU

Dear Mrs. Jackson,

No matter how difficult the problem, how trivial it may have seemed, how important or unimportant it was, you were always there to listen. Always with sincere interest and unfailing ideas, you Mrs. Jackson, continued to contribute to each student's well-being and future.

The many necessary exams you've arranged for our benefit have shown that you know best. Sometimes we were not as cooperative and respectful of your ideas as we should have been. However, now as time proceeds and situations alter our lives, we realize that the advice you give and have given us accounts tremendously for our standing now.

Mere thanks is not enough to express how grateful we are to you—one whose generosity and tactfulness have filled in the gaps of our lives. But, we're hoping that you'll read this tribute with the heart-felt realization that your Seniors past and present appreciate your dedication to our lives even though we may have acted otherwise.

Please accept these grateful "Thank You's" for they come from our hearts.
Thankfully,
The Senior Class of '67

SOURCE: *THE POINTER REVIEW, JUNE 1967*

Here)

Miss Davis was my homeroom teacher. She was really nice, a sweetheart. She was like a mother figure.

Joyce "Judy" Brown Crump
Class of 1956

Ms. Jackson was interested in you continuing your education. She had faith that you could do it and encouraged you. She would work diligently to find grant or scholarship money to make your college attendance possible.

Carolyn Garnett Epps
Class of 1966

VIRGINIA SCOTT JACKSON— MATHEMATICS AND SCIENCE

Virginia Scott Jackson

Mrs. V. S. Jackson was my homeroom teacher my senior year. She was clearly in charge—no one questioned her authority. She was very funny. If someone was misbehaving she would say, "If you don't sit down, I am going to hang you out the window by your pompadour."

When I was in the 10th grade, I took driver's ed; I believe Mr. Shelby Guss was our teacher. We learned to drive in a 1948 Chevy. Mrs. Jackson took the class with us. At the end of the semester, a person came from the DMV to give us our driving test. Mrs. Jackson crashed the car into a school bus. No one was hurt, and there was no damage, but she failed her test. I don't remember if she ever learned how to drive.

Emma Samuel Vaughan
Class of 1950

Mrs. Virginia Scott Jackson was my homeroom teacher; she was very funny. One day I accidentally said, "Yes, Sir" to her. She laughed and said, "I've been called many things, but never a sir."

Gladys Rich Ferguson
Class of 1941

CAROLYN BUNDY JOHNSON— MATHEMATICS

Carolyn Bundy Johnson

I graduated from Union High in 1945. I went to Virginia Union and graduated in 1949. After graduation, I went to live with an aunt in Pennsylvania and tried to get a job with the federal government. I took training with the federal government in taxes.

When I came home for a visit in the summer of 1950, they [Caroline School Board] were looking for teachers because all the men had been drafted. I accepted a position at St. James two-room school house teaching grades 4 through 7. I was also offered a job in Pennsylvania but decided to stay in Caroline because they needed teachers. I had to go back to school to take education classes at Virginia State College. I went for two summers for six weeks each summer to get my teacher's certificate. I taught at St. James for four years.

In 1954, Union High needed a math teacher. They had a person, but the person was not qualified. Superintendent Vaughan looked at my record and asked me to transfer to Union High. I transferred to Union High, and the other person went to St. James. I taught general math, general science, algebra I and II, geometry, and trigonometry. Besides teaching, I had homeroom and office duty where I counted the money that had been collected from selling books, the cafeteria, and so on. I was also a senior class sponsor.

I encouraged my students to make something out of themselves, to do more than their parents, to go a little further. I wanted them to believe that they could be somebody, be good citizens, go to college, and do something with their lives. My teaching days at Union High were good days; it was a pleasant experience.

Carolyn Bundy Johnson
Class of 1945
Mathematics Teacher

I took geometry from Mrs. Johnson. The counselor accidentally put about 10 students in the class who had not taken algebra. When Mrs. Johnson realized what had happened, she told us we could not take geometry without knowing algebra because algebra was a prerequisite for the class. She was able to adapt to the situation. She split the class into two groups and taught one group algebra, and the other group, geometry.

Catherine Ferguson
Class of 1969

GENEVA JOHNSON–
BUSINESS

Geneva Johnson

After graduating from Union High in 1963, I went to Virginia State and majored in business. I was inspired by Miss Easter and wanted to be a business teacher like her. I wanted to be a role model to children and let them know times were changing and there were other opportunities available to them that were not available in the past. I finished all my classes at Virginia State except my student teaching in 1967. While finishing up my requirements for graduation, I worked part-time at Caroline High and taught night classes at Union High.

I graduated from Virginia State in 1968. I had an opportunity to teach in North Carolina, but I turned it down. I was a home body and believed in giving back to my community; therefore, I wanted to teach in Caroline County. Also, my student loans had a clause that allowed a portion of the loan to be forgiven for every year that I worked in certain counties. Caroline County was one of the counties.

I started teaching business courses at Union High in 1968. Mr. Ruffin was responsible for me getting the position. I wanted to be a role model, the kind of person my teachers were to me, a source of encouragement, to give guidance, build the students' self-esteem and confidence. I wanted

them to know they could do what ever they put their minds to, not to let anyone make them feel less than, to reach for the stars.

I was fresh out of college and had taken a lot of method classes. I expected my students to do everything right and quickly learned my expectations were unrealistic. I had to adjust my expectations to deal with the reality. I expected my students to be respectful to me and other students. My goal was to help them become successful and to take away something that would help them have a livelihood. I wanted to teach them to be prepared for the work place; to know how to dress, use proper language, and understand the importance of body language; to make eye contact and develop a firm handshake.

Geneva Johnson Thompson
Class of 1963
Business Teacher

CHRISTOPHER C. LEE–
SCIENCE AND PHYSICS

Christopher C. Lee

Christopher C. Lee came to Union High 1951 to replace the science teacher, Virginia Scott Jackson, who died that summer. He taught general science, biology, chemistry, physics, and sometimes math. He wanted to be the students' friend. He wanted them to have a sense of belonging and to be all they could be in life. In addition to teaching science, he was a yearbook sponsor and member of the Finance Committee. He also worked with the students in the community. He was a Boy Scout leader and taught Sunday School.

Lee sought to challenge his students to work to the best of their abilities a help them develop the skills needed to become productive citizens and future leaders. While teaching at Union High, he reached out and helped many students better themselves. A lot of his students went on to college and higher education. They would come back and tell him how they appreciated his teaching because it helped them

35

in college. At one point, the superintendent of schools would receive letters for some colleges saying how well Lee had prepared students for college.

The extra duties he was required to perform at school took up too much of his time and did not allow him to devote as much time as he would like to teaching. He asked for more money and was denied. With a young and growing family to support, he took the federal service exam in 1969 and began to receive offers from government agencies. He left Union High in 1969 to work for the Social Security Administration.

FROM JEANETTA ROCK LEE (WIFE) AND NOTES WRITTEN BY MR. LEE

DR. WALTER E. LOWE– *Industrial Arts*

Dr. Walter E. Lowe

I am from Sussex County, Virginia. I attended Sussex County Training School up to the 10th grade and completed high school at Virginia State High School. I then attended Virginia State College and graduated in 1939. In May of my senior year, I applied for jobs in three different areas. Northern Virginia and Caroline County were two of the locations. I went to Northern Virginia for an interview and received favorable consideration but did not sign a contract. When I returned home, I had a letter asking me to contact the superintendent [Mr. W. A. Vaughan] of Caroline County Schools. I was working at Virginia Beach in the summer, and the superintendent was vacationing there. He interviewed me at Virginia Beach. I received offers from both Northern Virginia and Caroline County. I accepted the offer from Caroline County because I felt I could make more headway there. I came to Union High in August of 1939 as the first industrial arts teacher. I was paid $100 per month. Women teachers were paid $55 per month unless they had a specialty like home economics.

In addition to learning industrial arts, I wanted the students to develop a personality; to develop as an individual so that they could fit into society. I exposed them to my downfalls so that they could learn from my experiences. I wanted them to learn how to be responsible, intelligent, and knowledgeable, to participate in the society of which they were a part. I wanted them to become good citizens. I feel that I have done that. Many of my students have become teachers or contractors and made a good living.

I expected the students to participate to their highest ability. To help them do this, I hired many students to work for my contracting company while they were still students. I had as many as 12 students working for me at one time. Students were paid based on what they produced. I cleared it with the supervisor to verify I was not breaking any rules. During the school year, the students who could travel would work with me after school. School ended at 3 p.m.; no one started working until 3:30 p.m. I also hired students during the summer.

During the 1940s, I was eligible for the draft. A lot of the male teachers were getting drafted. Some teachers wanted to join the military. The superintendent asked me if I wanted to join the military. I said no because I had just gotten married. The superintendent got me a deferment because I was needed at the school. I had to teach additional classes that were added to the curriculum during the war. They were Fundamentals of Machines and Fundamentals of Industrial Training. The purpose of these courses was to prepare students for the military. Mostly boys took the classes; some girls took them, too.

In addition to teaching, I was the assistant principal from 1964 until 1969, director of transportation from 1959 until 1969, and director of athletics from 1940 through the early 1960s. I also coached baseball from 1939 until I became assistant principal and was basketball coach in the 1940s and 1950s. When I left, the school board hired three people to do all the jobs I had been doing.

My time at Union High was a valuable time for me. I learned about patrons of the school and students. It was a pleasant experience. I got along nicely with the teachers at Union High. We had a lot to do to move the students forward. We had to fight to get the students what they needed. Some teachers were afraid of getting involved because they did not want to lose their jobs. I was not afraid of losing my job because I had a my contracting business. If I lost my job, I still had my business. In general, we worked together to get what was best for the students.

Dr. Walter E. Lowe
Industrial Arts Teacher
Assistant Principal
Coach

DEDICATION

In recognition of his twenty-six years of dedicated and understanding service to our school and school community as a teacher, coach, advisor, builder, and friend, the senior class wishes to dedicate its humble effort here to MR. WALTER E. LOWE. His unselfish, loyal service to our school and country will forever serve as an inspiration to us to live a life of service—for a life of service is a life that counts.

THE SENIOR CLASS
SOURCE: *1965 UNION HIGH YEARBOOK*

OLA R. LUCK– LIBRARIAN

Ola R. Luck

When I finished Virginia State, I sent out applications and got several offers. I came to Union High in 1955 as the librarian. I picked Union High because I had two sisters who lived in Richmond.

I had the supplies I needed; we did not get used books. I was able to order new books as long as I stayed within my budget.

Study hall was held in the library. I did not allow the students to use it for social time. I told them they could talk on their own time after school. They were in study hall to study.

I was also the sponsor for the library club. I taught the children to become interested in reading. They would have contest to see who could read the most books. Students worked as library aides; they worked at the checkout desk and helped shelve books.

Union High was a very close-knit place. I made lifelong friends there. I met Ms. Rucker there in September 1955, and we are still friends today. I enjoyed my time at Union High.

Ola Luck
Librarian

Miss Ola Luck was my favorite person in the school. I could talk to her about anything. She was a very pleasant and friendly lady, but she was firm too. She would not allow students to get too noisy [in the library].

Sherrillyn LaVerne Smith Silver
Class of 1965

Ms. Luck, the librarian, was a classy lady. She would say, "The library is a reading room, not a chatting room."

Carolyn Garnett Epps
Class of 1966

JAMES LUCKIE–MATHEMATICS, GEOGRAPHY, AND PHYSICS

James E. Luckie

Mr. Luckie was my friend. He was hard on us. I was good at math and was studious. The students would tell me, "Mr. Luckie thinks everyone should be like you."

Carolyn Bundy Johnson
Class of 1945
Mathematics Teacher

Mr. Luckie taught math. I never saw anyone write on the board so fast. He was very smart. He was teaching below his abilities; he should have been teaching at a college.

He told us the next comet would come in 1972. We were all laughing, but it did. The comet came through. He was a nice person to get along with, but he did not take any foolishness or playing. He would send students to the office.

Jesse Jackson
Class of 1947

I took algebra from Mr. Luckie. He was very smart. He would write on the blackboard with one hand and erase with the other hand. He had taught my older sister, Daisy Jackson (she was known as Fret Jackson at Union High), who was good at math. I was not very good at math. Mr. Luckie expected me to be good at math because my sister was. One day I raised my hand in class to ask a question. Mr. Luckie told me I did not need to be in his class because I could not keep up. He said my sister could keep up, so he did not see why I could not keep up. After that day, he stopped calling my name when he called the roll. After about the third day, I asked him why he did not call my name, and he said I was no longer in his class. I was very embarrassed and humiliated. I started to cry and went to the cafeteria (where

my mother worked) to tell my mother. My mother and I went to the office, and I was put in Mr. Beverly's algebra class.

Beryl Jackson
Attended Union High 1963–1965
Graduated from Caroline High in 1968

I took geometry from Mr. Luckie. He was a genius; he knew his math. He would write so fast he would break the chalk. He loved to teach. He was smart and would get flustered if students did not understand.

Beulah Collins
Class of 1959

I took algebra from Mr. Luckie. He would assign all the girls to sit on the front row; no boys. He would write so hard and fast that chalk particles would fly. You had to pay attention because he would go so fast. He was very smart but not very patient. Students would have to go to the board to solve problems. You had to get the answer fast, or he would make you go sit down and call someone else.

Sherrillyn LaVerne Smith Silver
Class of 1965

I took several mathematics courses from Mr. Luckie. He was a genius. He would write on the board so fast that he broke the chalk. He had us students competing to complete problems. About four or five students would go to the blackboard and compete to be the first to solve a problem. It wasn't enough to get the right answer—you had to get the right answer as fast as possible.

Williabel Jones Davis
Class of 1966

Mr. Luckie knew math. He would write on the board and erase at the same time. He felt the students should keep up with him. He would get upset if they did not.

Vivian Garnett Coleman
Class of 1953

Mr. Luckie took a lot of pictures of the students. He would put the pictures on the bulletin board in his room to note student accomplishments. This made students feel good about their accomplishments.

Aterita Baker Brown
Attended Union High from 1958 to 1961

I was terrified of Mr. Luckie. I had never seen a teacher so animated, like a jack rabbit. He would write on the board so fast, the chalk would break and pieces of chalk and chalk dust would fly everywhere. If you sat in the front of the class you would get chalk dust on you.

Joyce "Judy" Brown Crump
Class of 1957

KATIE M. POOLE–ENGLISH

At the beginning of my senior year, we had to fill out forms for the yearbook with our ambitions and so on. I said I wanted to be an airline stewardess. One teacher told me that was not a reasonable expectation for a Black girl, so I wrote down secretary, which made me feel like I had to settle. That was before I met Mrs. Poole.

My English literature teacher, Mr. Austin, left in the middle of the school year and was replaced by Mrs. Poole, who taught the class for the second half of the semester. Mrs. Poole was relatively young and dressed very elegantly. She wore nice dresses with scarves and the like. I would think, "I want to be like her when I grow up."

One day she overheard some girls in the class talking about getting married. She asked the girls, "What do you plan to do besides get married and have babies?" They did not really have an answer.

TO MR. JAMES E. LUCKIE
A DEDICATED TEACHER

Mr. Luckie was born in Atlanta, Georgia, and educated in the public schools there. Upon graduation from high school, he entered Morris Brown College in Atlanta, where he earned a B.S. degree in mathematics; he also attended Hampton Institute and Virginia Union University.

Mr. Luckie came to Union High School in February, 1942, from Mississippi. His versatility and usefulness have helped the progress of the students and the school in numerous ways.

His enormous knowledge extends into many different areas of education, mathematics and science, photography, electronics, music, religions, and twelve different languages.

"Each human being has a gift, a talent, secreted in the depths of his being which is his special contribution to life. Through spiritual blindness you may not know or be aware of your own gift but it is there, ready and waiting for the magic key to turn in the lock—for that moment to arrive when you will cry, 'This, then is my gift to life !'

"If this gift is only the gift of humble service, do not despair—rejoice, for this is the gift of perfect love."

The Class of 1964 wishes to acknowledge with gratitude the untiring efforts of this teacher to instill knowledge, discipline, and to build character. In appreciation, we dedicate our humble appreciation here to the past, present, and future services rendered to the Union High School and the school community. Long may you live, long may you lead, long may you serve.

SOURCE: 1964 UNION HIGH YEARBOOK

She told the class, "We are not going to have English literature today. We are going to have a life talk." She gave all the boys passes to go to the library so she could just talk to the girls. She talked to us about dating, what to look for in a man, why we should not get married young, not settling, stepping out, and doing something not expected.

In Caroline County, the only jobs available to Black girls were working in a restaurant, housekeeping, or cooking. Because of Mrs. Poole's talk I was encouraged to leave Caroline County. I remembered whenever I called my friend, Lavern Smith, her mother would say I had a good speaking voice and tell me I would make a good phone operator. After I graduated, I moved to Washington, D.C., and applied for a position with the phone company. I started out as a phone operator, and when I retired 30 years later, I was an executive office manager. After I retired from the phone company at age 50, I became a flight attendant for SkyTrek (a charter airline company in Richmond, Virginia). I worked there for 2 years and quit when the company moved to Newark, New Jersey. Mrs. Poole was only at Union High for one-half a semester (she is not even in the yearbook), but I attribute all my success to that talk she gave us that one day.

Eleanor Thomas Hawkins
Class of 1965

Eleanor Thomas Hawkins (right) and SkyTrek coworker. Courtesy Eleanor Thomas Hawkins.

ARLETHA QUASH RUCKER– GEOGRAPHY AND SOCIAL STUDIES

Arletha Quash Rucker

Mrs. Rucker taught me geography. She was such a lady. She was always impeccably dressed (perfect makeup). She was very serious about her subject and expected her students to be serious, too. She gave us a lot of work, and she expected a lot from us. She had high expectations of all students (whether A, B, C, or D students). F's failed. There was no social promotion in those days.

Williabel Jones Davis
Class of 1966

BLONNIE TIPTON– BAND

Blonnie Tipton

I taught music from the 1959–1960 school year through the 1963–1964 school year. Before coming to Union High, I taught music and other subjects at Walker Grant High School in Fredericksburg. I took the position at Union High because I only had to teach band.

I felt I had to be a good role model. I encouraged the students to do well in all their subjects, not just music, and to express themselves intelligently. Many of the students lived with their grandparents, or their parents were away. I would listen to their problems and help them.

I expected my students to practice in order to be good players and develop skills. They had practice charts where they had to record their practice time and get their parents' signature. I wanted them to really learn to play and enjoy the music. I had inspections to make sure they were neat and clean—shoes shined, hair neat, and so on. I told them, "You must sound good, look good, and do a good job."

I wanted to give them a good experience, to learn to play and enjoy music. I wanted them to continue to play after high school and pass it on to their children. Music gives discipline that will teach you to do well in life. I would see students later in life, and they would tell me what a positive impact being in the band had on their lives.

One of the challenges I had was getting students to stay after school for practice. Students came to school by bus, so it was hard for them to stay after school. After about a year, I was able to get students to practice after school. The parents were very helpful. They would pick up a group of students and take them home. I would drop students off who lived along the way on my way home [Fredericksburg]. Sometimes I would take a student home with me.

I felt I had sufficient supplies. The school, Band Boosters, or PTA all provided what I needed. The school bought the large instruments, the percussion instruments, and the music. The students had to purchase the small instruments. If a student could not purchase an instrument, we would loan them an instrument.

Parents did a lot of fundraising. They would sell light bulbs and candy. Parents did great and were happy to do it. Parents had a desire for their children and grandchildren to have better opportunities than they did. They were very proud of the band and happy to support it. The better the band did, the more support we received.

As I look back at my tenure at Union High, one of the most memorable moments was when I took two bands, the high school band and the elementary band, to march in the Memorial Day Parade in Fredericksburg in May 1963. One of the highlights of my teaching career was teaching at Union High. I still keep in touch with some of the students. I have many fond memories and good feelings about the students and teachers.

I would like to be remembered as a person who was interested in the total student. I gave them the best I had to offer. I tried to be giving and compassionate and help the students be successful in whatever they chose to do.

Blonnie Tipton
Band Teacher

Mrs. Tipton was a disciplinarian and very knowledgeable about music. She was also very strict about appearance. The band uniform always had to be neat, clean, and pressed. The shoes were white bucks, and they were to be clean at all times. There could be no white polish on the red soles and no red on the white portion of the shoe.

Mrs. Tipton was also a very caring person. Band met after school, and on several occasions I could not get a ride home. There were parents that often gave us rides that lived in the community. When this happened I would start walking the 7 miles home and often would be picked up in route. Mrs. Tipton would give students a ride home and took me to her residence on several occasions. I stayed in contact with Mrs. Tipton years after graduating from Union High. I went to Howard University, majoring in music education, and became a band director.

William Brawner
Class of 1966

Our band teacher, Mrs. Bonnie Tipton, was a perfectionist. Mrs. Tipton taught me to play the trumpet and the baritone horn (in treble clef). We had a marching band and a concert band. We went to All-State. We played Sousa marches, Bach, Beethoven, and Tchaikovsky and Big Band-era music.

Williabel Jones Davis
Class of 1966

Mrs. Tipton was a sincere, dedicated and focused teacher. She had a lot of rules that students were expected to follow.

Vernelle Twiggs
Class of 1967

Mrs. Tipton taught us the importance of building a solid foundation. She would instruct us to practice difficult music slowly until we learned the music and build up to the fast tempo. This skill helped us tackle any difficult situation in life. Mrs. Tipton was meticulous and demanding. She did not tolerate her students being tardy or unprepared. Students were expected to memorize the music and steps and had to audition before each performance. If they were not prepared, they were not allowed to perform.

Beryl Jackson
Attended Union High from 1963 to 1965
Graduated from Caroline High in 1968

NATHAN WASHINGTON– FRENCH

I was on the yearbook staff. Mr. Washington was the yearbook sponsor. We had to select people for the Hall of Fame. In the past, the popularity contest winners were relegated to a small clique of people. Mr. Washington talked to us about what a popularity contest

Nathan Washington

really was because he wanted the selections to be fair. I was voted most popular [girl]. I was very popular. I had known most people in the school since we were in elementary. However, I do not feel I would have won if Mr. Washington had not been an advocate for me.

Carolyn Jackson
Class of 1961

Mr. Washington would come to the cafeteria and have students tell him what they were eating in French. Students would see him coming into the cafeteria and leave out the other door.

Gladys Fitzhugh-Pemberton
Class of 1964

Mr. Washington would assign each person a French name. We had to use that name in class for the entire school year; my name was Cecile. He would divide the class into groups and give up conversations to memorize and perform in front of the class.

Sherrillyn LaVerne Smith Silver
Class of 1965

Mr. Washington was my French teacher. I had two years of French from him. I credit him with my success in the two years of French that were required of me in college. I also feel that he laid such a good foundation that when I studied French in Paris, where in that classroom only French was spoken, I was able to not only survive but thrive.

Williabel Jones Davis
Class of 1966

RUTH YOUNG WILSON– MUSIC AND ENGLISH

Mrs. Ruth Wilson was a good choir director. She wanted the best from students and worked with students to help them to develop to their potential.

Carolyn Jackson
Class of 1961

Ruth Young Wilson

Mrs. Wilson taught English and Music. She had a profound affect on me. She exposed me to all types of music. It was such a good experience, I love music today.

Barbara Jones Rock
Class of 1961

Mrs. Ruth Y. Wilson was a fantastic choir director. We performed music from Broadway musicals like *West Side Story* and *The Sound of Music*. Mrs. Wilson taught us four-part harmony. She would rehearse each section separately and then put everything together. She was very meticulous and a perfectionist. She expected us to sing on key with perfect pitch and make beautiful music with our voices, and of course, we did.

Williabel Jones Davis
Class of 1966

LORENZA YOUNG–COMMERCIAL SCIENCE

Lorenza Young

I was the first business teacher. I taught commercial science (typing and shorthand) from September 1949 through June 1950. I came to Union High after graduating from Hampton Institute. The classroom was equipped with 20 new typewriters and typing tables. In addition to teaching commercial science, I was also required to perform secretarial work for Mr. Ruffin for two periods.

Lorenza Young Robinson
Commercial Science Teacher

I took typing and shorthand from Miss Young. She was very interested in her students. She was an excellent teacher who shared her skills and knowledge.

Dorothy Samuels Jackson
Class of 1950

SECRETARIES

Norma Guss

Rebecca Wright

Thelma Williams

Jeanetta Rock Lee

Thelma Jackson

Essie Williams

Doris Rock Carter

Julie Jones

OTHER STAFF

*Custodians (l. to r.)
Vincent H. Childs,
Clyde F. Johnson Jr.*
SOURCE: 1968 UNION HIGH
YEARBOOK

*Cafeteria staff (l. to r.)
Ora Hutchinson, Nettie
Saunders, Ester Boone,
Mable Jackson.*
SOURCE: 1965 UNION HIGH YEAR-
BOOK.

School bus drivers. SOURCE: 1962 UNION HIGH YEARBOOK.

Administration and Faculty Summary[43]

J. T. Abercrombie ....Masonry

Eugene A. Austin..English, French

Mary B. Banks ....Home Economics

A. McKee Banks ....Agriculture

Bettie Banks ....Music

Edward K. Barksdale ....Physical Education

James Barrett Jr...English

Muriel Washington Bennett..............................Librarian

Commodore Nathaniel (C.N.) Bennett ....History

Claudia Beverly ....Business Education

Reginald Beverly ....Mathematics, Science

Pauline Shelton Boxley......................................Home Economics (substitute)

Lloyd Boxley ....Agriculture

Bernice Branch ....Cosmetology

Leroye Bray ....Barbering

James A. Brewington ....Physical Education, Coach

Mason Brooks ....Mathematics

Ruth M. Brown...Physical Education

Richard Burnett...Band

Pearl G. Carr ....French

Louise Byrd Carter ....English, French, Choir Director

Charles A. Carter...English

Ruby Carter...Commerce

William Carter ....English

Robert Cashwell ....Science, Coach

Wilbur Chance..Science, English

Edward Chester...Biology, Physical Education

Frederick E. Corpening ....Science

Mildred J. Corpening ....English

Mary Quash Cummings ....Librarian

Archie W. Dabney..Physical Education

Mary Ellen White Dungee ....History, English, Government

Beryl Fortune ....Physical Education

William Galloway..Masonry

Administration and Faculty Summary (continued)

Rosa Graves...Business Education

J. Shelby Guss ....Government

Mary Ann Hanna...English

Mildred Easter Harris ....Commerce, Business Education

William Hay III ....English

Lena Hicks ....Science

John L. Hicks ....Mathematics, Science, Coach

Elizabeth D Holden ....Civics

Marguerite Davis Jackson ....English, Guidance Counselor

Virginia Scott Jackson....................................Mathematics, Science

Theresa T. Jackson..English

William Jennings..Band

Carolyn Bundy Johnson ....Mathematics

Geneva Johnson ....Business Education

E. M. Kornegay ....English

Leon A. Lawrence..Mathematics

Christopher C. Lee ....Science, Physics

Dr. Walter E. Lowe ....Industrial Arts, Assistant Principal

Fraulein Lowe ....Guidance Counselor

M. E. Lownes ....Mathematics

Bernice Lucas ....Commerce

Ola R. Luck ....Librarian

James Luckie ....Mathematics, Geography, Physics

William Mason...English

Naomi Miller...English, History, Mathematics

Charlotte A. Nichols.......................................Business Education

Walter Penney ....Health, Physical Education, Biology

Lorraine Pettie...Commerce

Ruth Morton Barksdale Phillips.......................History, Government, English

Katie M. Poole ....Commercial Science

Sherley E. Porter ....Mathematics

Allie Ragin..Geography, Civics

Celestine Coleman Ragland ....Home Economics

Earl Richards...Physical Education, Coach

Rosa Riddick ....Commercial Foods

Administration and Faculty Summary *(continued)*

G. Y. Robertson ....Commerce

Arletha Quash Rucker ....Geography, Social Studies

George B. Ruffin ....Principal, History, Coach

I. D. Ruffin ....Music

Latina L. Satterwhite ....English

Rexall Stafford ....Physical Education

Deloris Stiff ....Physical Education

Alma Stills..Business Education

Doris H. Swinton ....Physical Education

Jewel A. Taylor ....Music

Blonnie Tipton ....Band

Martha L. Travis ....Physical Education

Doris M. Upshur ....Business Education

David Walker ....Biology, Coach

Blanche Lomax Washington ....Social Studies

Nathan Washington Jr. ....French, History

Walter Webb ....Mathematics, Chemistry, Physics, Coach

John Wenderoth...Distributive Education

James White..Masonry

D. L. Williams ....French

James Williams...French, English

Ruth Young Wilson ....Music, English

Charlotte Young ....English

Hovey Rice Young ....Principal, Latin, Civics, Social Problems

Lorenza C. Young...Commercial Science

Walter Young ....English, History

Student Life

Despite their common racial classification of Negro or Colored, the Union High student population came from diverse backgrounds. Their physical appearance was a testament to their varied ancestry. They were the descendants of European settlers, Africans slaves and freemen, Native Americans, or some combination of the three. Some Rappahannock Indians took umbrage to be classified as Negro and fought hard to maintain their Indian identification. A few refused induction in the Colored unit of the segregated U.S. Army during World War II and requested to serve with Whites. Their request was denied, and they were convicted and sentenced to two years in federal prison for violating the Selective Service Act.[44]

In the 1950s and 1960s several Rappahannock Indians took steps to prevent their children from being required to attend Negro schools. In 1954, they requested a separate school in the Central Point-Alps community for their children.[45] They petitioned again in 1963.[46] On advice from the Department of Education, the school board determined that the number of Indian children in the county did not justify constructing a separate school.[47] The group of Rappahannock Indians then requested tuition grants and transportation to send their children to the Sharon Indian School in King William County. Both the King William County and Caroline County School Boards indicated they could not justify the expenditure.[48]

The educational level of the parents of Union High students ranged from no formal education to college education. Regardless of the parents' educational level, most students lived in a household where at least one parent or adult valued education and saw it as the way for self-improvement.

Here

The occupations of the students' parents also varied, which led to a range of economic backgrounds. Union High students were the children of sharecroppers, manual laborers, domestic workers, teachers, ministers, government workers, and business owners. Because job opportunities in Caroline County were limited, the parents of some Union High students worked in areas outside of the county such as Fredericksburg, Richmond, Northern Virginia, and Washington, D.C. Some commuted to these locations daily, others lived there during the week and returned to Caroline County on the weekend, and others moved permanently and left their children in the care of grandparents or other relatives in Caroline County.

Many students worked while they were in school or during the summer. Some toiled on the family farm or business. Other students labored to help pay household expenses or to pay college tuition for their siblings. Some students worked to have money for their school expenses, others, to have pocket money.

Enrollment at Union High continued to grow every year, but many students left before they received their diplomas. The graduating class often consisted of less than half the number of students who started with the class in the 8th grade. For example, in 1946 the 8th grade class consisted of 120 students.[49] The class size decreased each school year, with 63 students graduating in 1950.[50]

Students left school for a variety of reasons: to work full-time to support themselves or their families, to work on the family farm or business, to get married and start a family, or to relocate to an area outside the county with their families. During war time, some students left to join the military either because they were drafted or volunteered. Some students who left school did later obtain their high school diplomas.

Although most Union High alumni view their time as Union High as positive, some did recall some negative experiences. Some students felt some teachers showed favoritism to students based on their skin color, the community in which they lived, their family economic status, athletic ability, or parental involvement in the school.

Union High students were born into a segregated world, and for most, segregation was the only life they knew. The general consensus seemed to be that the races got along in Caroline County as long as the Blacks stayed in their place. When asked how they felt about attending a segregated school, most alumni stated that growing up they did not feel they were at a disadvantage. School was a safe haven where they were nurtured and cared for and felt protected.

Despite their varied backgrounds, these students all became part of the Union High family and for the most part had a very pleasant experience. Many students formed lifelong friendships and found marriage partners at Union High.

TRANSPORTATION AND LIVING ARRANGEMENTS

Union High was located in Bowling Green, Virginia (marked with a star on map) . Students had to travel great distances to attend school.

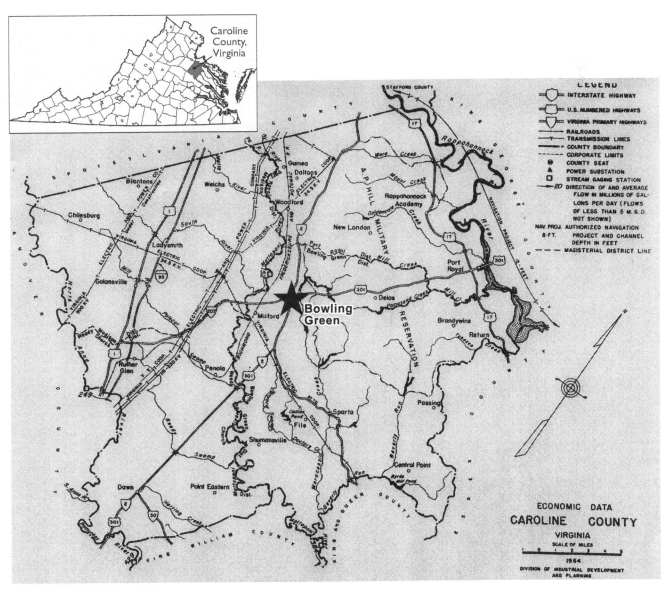

I lived in Bowling Green; we did not have any school buses. We walked 5 miles each way to school each day. We would leave the house at 7 a.m. and get to school at 9 a.m. We would leave school at 3:30 p.m. and get home about 5 p.m. Then we would work in the field, picking peas and shucking corn until the sun went down. We would eat our supper, get our lessons, and go to bed.

Carrie Myers Saunders
Class of 1932

I lived in the dormitory with three other boys: Stanley Jones, Thomas Jones (they were first cousins), and Samuel Courtney. We had to pay $14 for room and board. The principal, Rev. Hovey Young, was from Kilmarnock, Lancaster County; he lived in the dorm, too.

Reginald A. Beverly
Class of 1933
Mathematics Teacher

When I first started school, I lived in the old dormitory. We moved to the new dormitory around 1935. There were five girls living in the dormitory: me, Viola Miller (my sister), and three other girls. Some of the teachers lived there, too. Mrs. Virginia Scott Jackson was in charge of the dorm. Miss Louise Byrd and Mrs. Mayme Coleman, the industrial supervisor, stayed in the dormitory when she was visiting from Richmond, Virginia. There were two boys in the boy's dormitory: Hill Beverly and Charles Ragland.

Vergie Miller
Class of 1938

I lived in Dawn. I stayed in the dormitory during the week. My parents would drive me to school on Monday and pick me up on Friday. I stayed in the old dormitory at the beginning of my freshman year and then moved to the new dormitory. Other students in the dorm were Viola Miller, Vergie Miller (sisters), Nellie Jones, and Delia Gray. There was no privacy in the old dormitory. Everyone slept in one big room on the second floor.

There was a faculty dining room, student dining room, and kitchen on the first floor.

We moved to the new dormitory before it was completed. The first floor was not completely finished. I believe we moved in the winter because I remember the boys having to bring in wood. In the new dormitory, the sleeping area was on the second floor, and there were separate rooms—two girls to a room. The principal had an office on the first floor, and the auditorium was there, too.

Rosa Bell Courtney Quash
Class of 1940

My older brothers and sisters were among those who relied on makeshift modes of transportation to get them to school. They traveled first by mule and buggy and then by a pickup truck converted to a school bus. When his oldest child had finished 7th grade at St. John Elementary School and became eligible to enter high school, Rev. Willie J. Wright, our distant cousin, made his truck into a school bus to transport not only his own children but as many other children as his bus could accommodate to Union High School. He erected a canvas top over the body of the truck and fixed long benches along its sides for seating. That crude contraption enabled many children who otherwise would not have been able to do so to continue their education beyond the seventh grade.

Getting to the school bus was no easier for the children from my neighborhood than walking the two and a half miles to St. John Elementary School had been. We left home around 7:30 a.m. and arrived at Union High, about 7 miles away, around 9:00 a.m. Our well-worn path took us through a dense forest, past a gristmill and a millpond, across a footbridge, onto a hard surface highway, and, finally, to the bus stop. We waited for the bus at a small general store. When the weather was inclement, we were allowed to wait inside the store. Occasionally, we missed the school bus and either walked or hitchhiked to school. We were not about to return home because we knew that a plenty of work would be waiting to be done. We took our time getting to school, often not arriving there before noon.[51]

> *Florence Coleman Bryant*
> *Class of 1940*

I lived in Naulkala and Supply. It was the same place; the name of the area was changed after they built AP Hill.[52] We had to walk 3 miles to the bus stop, which was Pitts Store at Passing, Virginia. The bus ride was about an hour. We would leave the house around 7 a.m. and get to school around 9 a.m. After school, we would do it all in reverse. We would get home around 4:30 and do our chores (chop wood, bring it in the house, etc.) until it got dark. We would eat supper, do the dishes, and do our homework at the kitchen table by lamplight. After we finished our homework, we would get ready for the next day and go to bed.

> *Carolyn Bundy Johnson*
> *Class of 1945*
> *Mathematics Teacher*

In the late 1930s, my grandfather [Louis T. Washington] brought a bus and used it to take children to school. He had two buses, but he only used one at a time. He had to get a contract from the county, but he owned the buses. My father [Thomas Jackson] drove the bus. Before AP Hill, the bus would start at Mica, go to Baylorstown, Bowling Green, and then school. After we moved when AP Hill was built, the bus started at Woodford, went to Guinea, Snell, Paige, Bowling Green, and then school.

Mr. Clavon Bates would also drive the bus if my father was not available. My mother [Carrie Jackson] would drive sometimes, too. I believe she was the first female bus driver in the county. When I started Union High in 1943, my father drove the bus for the first and second years. Then my older brother, Leonza, started driving. He was a junior in high school. Eventually the bus had other drivers.

> Jesse Jackson
> Class of 1947

My cousins Lucille Burruss, her sister Arlene Burruss (passed Jan 2009), Evelyn Burruss, and Beverly Johnson walked 2 miles, and I walked 3 miles to get the bus to go to Union High School. The bus for White kids passed our homes to pick them up at their gates. They yelled out the windows "niggers" and spit on us as they passed. Betty Taylor, who lived nearby, was the only nice White kid to us. She always spoke and waved and still does to this day. We liked her very much and still do. We wanted an education and did not mind walking through the rain, snow, and sleet to get it. My first two years at high school, I never missed a day and only missed four days for the next two years. My cousin Lucille Burruss only missed two days for her entire four years.

> *Bert Twiggs Nichols*
> *Class of 1948*

I lived in Balty. We had to walk 3 1/2 to 4 miles to get to the bus stop, which was at my grandmother's house. The bus would cross the railroad tracks. The school buses for the White students did not cross the railroad tracks because it was dangerous. The bus ride was about 5 1/2 miles. We left the house at 7 a.m. and got to school about 8:45 a.m.

> *Jeanetta Rock Lee*
> *Class of 1952*
> *Secretary*

Jackson Hill was a community off of state route 17, south of Port Royal, Virginia. Students ready to go to high school had to go to the high school in Bowling Green. The county was not providing transportation for Blacks. The bus was owned by Mack Gray (my grandfather) that picked up those students in Jackson Hill, Virginia, (which was taken over by the government for Fort AP Hill) Port Royal, Supply, and many other small communities in what was then called The Area, denoting places taken over by the government. Most of the students spent a long time on the bus going to school and returning home. There was no heat on the buses at that time.

Mabel Gray [Mack Gray's daughter], was the first bus driver to pick up the children from Jackson Hill. She was my mother, Mabel Gray. [Earl Gray and Thornton Thurston also drove the bus.] Earl Gray was her brother. Thurston Thornton was the husband of Anna Thornton [daughter of Mack Gray aka Marie Gray Thornton; full name is Anna Marie Gray Thornton.]

Daisy Jackson Thomas
Class of 1950

I lived in Lent, Virginia, which is 3 miles from Port Royal. The first and second year of high school, Mr. Mac Gray owned a bus. He allowed the bus to be used to take children to school. The parents paid him so their children could ride the bus. His son, Earl Gray, and son-in-law, Thurston Thornton, took turns driving the school bus. The bus ride was about 15 miles and took about 50 minutes. The third and fourth year the county gave the children a bus. I had to walk 1 1/2 miles to the bus stop. The bus stop was located at the crossroads where John Wilkes Booth was killed. The bus ride was about 24 miles and took about 1 1/2 hours.

Gladys Rich Ferguson
Class of 1941

I lived in Chilesburg. In the 1940s, there was no school bus for Cedon. My Aunt, Mabel Brown, would stay with us during the week so she could catch the bus to Union High. Another friend who lived in Cedon, Magdaline Jones, would catch the Greyhound bus from Cedon to Ladysmith everyday and then catch the school bus to Union High.

Virginia Gray Latney
Class of 1958

William Quash. *Courtesy Irene Quash Fields.*

I lived in Dawn. The community did not get bus transportation until 1937. After my oldest sister graduated from the 7th grade, she went to New York to live with our aunt and attend high school.

During the mid 1930s, my father, William Quash—along with Wortham Fields and Lewis Tillman—would go to the school board and request transportation for the Black students. The school board would refuse their request. In 1937, the school board finally agreed to pay for a bus body but told them they would have to go to North Carolina to pick it up. Wortham Fields purchased a chassis and attached two milk crates to it to use for seats. He and his son, Malcolm, sat on the milk crates in the open air and drove the chassis to Raleigh, North Carolina, to pick up the bus body. They then drove back to Caroline County.

My two older brothers never attended high school because there was no transportation to the high school when they finished elementary school. By the time transportation was provided, they had already started working and did not want to stop. My other sister was the first person in my family to attend Union High. She started in 1937 and graduated in 1941.

Irene Quash Fields
Class of 1947

Wortham Fields. COURTESY IRENE QUASH FIELDS.

Lewis Tilman Sr. COURTESY MARY TILMAN PRICE.

I walked 2 miles to the bus stop, which was the Bowling Green Post Office. There was one bus stop for the Black and White students because buses for both Caroline and Union stopped there. The bus stop was segregated—Blacks on one side, Whites on the other. We were the last bus stop. Students living south of Bowling Green had to walk to Union.

Daisy Jackson Thomas
Class of 1950

In the early years [1940s], the school board worked out the bus routes and then would accept bids from people. The contracts had to be bid on every year. Before consolidation [closing of the one- and two-room school houses and moving students to the large brick building], the school buses were only used by Union High students. After consolidation, the elementary school children also rode the school bus.

In the mid- or early 1950s, the superintendent gave me the responsibility of mapping out the bus routes for the school buses carrying the Black children. I was not given a title or any additional pay for this responsibility. In Black education, teachers had to do a lot more to get the students what they needed. I did not mind the additional responsibility because it allowed me to map out bus routes that were better for the children. Before

[I was given the responsibility of mapping out the routes] some children had to walk a long way to get to their bus stop. I changed that.

After I had mapped out the routes, I would publicize the routes through the Black churches. (Back then we used the churches to communicate information.) People would submit their bids to the superintendent, who decided who would be given each route. The people who applied for the routes had to have their own chassis. After they were awarded the contract, the school board with give them the body. If the person lost the contract, they had to return the body. Some people who bid owned their buses. At some point the school board did away with contracts and began to purchase the buses and hire the bus drivers.

In addition to mapping out the bus routes, I was responsible for keeping the drivers up to date on the school bus routes. Students and teachers were allowed to drive the buses. They had to have a valid driver's license to be hired. After they were hired, they had to go to the DMV and get a license to drive a bus. Students were paid less than the adults. Teachers were paid for being a bus driver in addition to teaching. Some bus drivers could take the bus home. Other drivers would go to a certain location and pick up the bus. Buses driven by teachers and students were parked at the school while they were at school. If the bus had to go to the garage to be worked on by the mechanic, the driver would take the bus to the garage and get a ride back to school. (The garage was only about a mile from the school).

When I first was given the responsibility of mapping out the bus routes, I still had a full schedule teaching industrial arts, in addition to this responsibility. Sometimes I would be called to the office while I was teaching to talk to someone from the school board about a transportation matter. Around the late 1950s, I was given the title of director of transportation, and my teaching schedule was reduced. I was still not given any additional pay. I keep this position until I left the school system.

Dr. Walter E. Lowe
Industrial Arts Teacher
Assistant Principal
Coach

I lived in Dawn. I would leave my house around 7 a.m. and walk 5 to 6 miles to the bus stop at Dyson's store. We rode the bus to Shumansville and got off the bus at the elementary school. The bus would then travel through the neighborhood and pick up the children who attended Shumansville elementary. When the bus returned, we would get on the bus again and travel to Union High.

The bus did not have any heat. In the winter, when we arrived at homeroom, students would stand around the tin barrels that were used to burn wood to heat the class room to get warm. We would repeat the trip in reverse in the evening, often arriving at home around 5 or 5:30 p.m. In the winter, it would be dark, and we would have just enough time to eat dinner, do our homework by oil lamp, and go to bed.

Susie Carter Quash
Class of 1947

My cousins Franklin Minor and Curtis Wright were bus drivers. My last year, I asked Mr. Ruffin if I could become a bus driver. He said he would talk to Superintendent Vaughan. I had to take a driving test. My bus route was in Cedon. I would drive to Cedon, get the bus, drive my route, and park the bus at school. Sometimes I would take the bus home. When I started, I was paid $42 a month. Later on, I was paid $52 a month.

Waverly Minor
Class of 1962

I was a student bus driver. In order to be a bus driver, you had to be 18 years old and obtain a chauffeur's license. I was an assistant bus driver in my junior year. I drove the bus when the bus driver was not available. I had my own bus route my senior year. The school board owned the bus. I lived in Chilesburg. I would pick up students for Madison Elementary and Union High. I would drop the elementary school students off at Madison and continue to Union High. I parked the bus at school when I was at school. After school, I would drive the same bus route and take the bus home when I was finished. I think I was paid $2 a day.

Rudolph Gray
Class of 1964

I lived in Hewlett (now called Ruther Glen) on the Jericho Road side. I had about a 45-minute bus ride to school. The bus went through Jericho, McDuff, and Milford. We had a student bus driver. Three Devils Jump Road in Milford had three hills. When we got to the road the bus driver would sometimes speed over the hills, and the bus would leave the ground, especially when John Moore was driving.

Eleanor Thomas Hawkins
Class of 1965

I lived in Bowling Green. William Boone was our bus driver. He was a student and lived in Milford. My bus took two loads of students to school. In the morning, the bus would drop off the first load and come back and get us. In the afternoon, the bus would take the people who lived the furthest away from home first, come back and get the people who lived closer to the school.

Beryl Jackson
Attended Union High from 1963–1965
Graduated from Caroline High in 1968

I lived in Ruther Glen. My father, Reginald Arthur Beverly, taught at Union High. My mother, the late Bessie J. Beverly, taught at Union Elementary. I was lucky. Sometimes I rode the school bus that my father drove, and sometimes I rode to school in the car with my mother. Union High and Union Elementary were side by side. When I rode the school bus, the route was about an hour and a half long. We picked up students all along the road, and when students from different household lived near a store, they all walked to the store to be picked up. That was always an exciting stop because back then, we sometimes were allowed to go in the store to buy snacks.

Katrina Beverly Gill
Class of 1968

TYPICAL DAY

When we arrived at school the boys and girls were not allowed to play together on the playground. The girls played on one side, and the boys played on the other.

Gladys Rich Ferguson
Class of 1941

When students arrived at school they would line up according to grade level (1st grade–11th grade). The principal would pass out information (notices, etc.) to the students. The students entered the building by grade (1st , 2nd, 3rd, and so on) and went to their classrooms. There was devotion, Pledge of Allegiance, roll call, collect lunch money (from students who did not bring their lunch from home). Then we went to classes. Each subject was in a different room with different teachers.

For lunch, there was a cafeteria in the basement of the building where the chapel was located. Mrs. Lucy Paige Monte was the cook. She also cooked for Mr. Ruffin. Mr. George Davis owned a store on the school property. The students would go to his store and buy snacks. They were not allowed to leave the school property. At the end of the day, we returned to homeroom and were dismissed.

Clara Latney Hudson
Class of 1949

The bell would ring at 9:00 a.m., we would line up by grades in front of the school, the flag would be raised, and we would pledge allegiance to the American flag. We would enter the building. The boys would go up their steps, which were at the front door. The girls' steps were at the back door. We went directly to our homerooms.

Each grade had a different homeroom teacher. There were 8a, 8b, 8c, and 8d. They were the largest class. As students dropped out, there were fewer homerooms per class. By the time we were seniors, we had one homeroom teacher, Mrs. Virginia Scott Jackson. She was the only science teacher that the school had. We had about 10–15 minutes for homeroom.

In homeroom, there were devotions, which were Bible verses and prayer. After devotions, the announcements for the day were made. Then roll call and lunch money was collected. The highlight of homeroom for seniors came at the end of our year, the day Mrs. Jackson posted class ratings on the blackboard.

The bell would ring, and our day would begin with first period. There were six periods per day including lunch; the bell would ring at the end of each class.

The lunchroom was in the bottom of the building where the auditorium was located. Food was cooked fresh. Mrs. Nettie Saunders was one of the cooks. Everyone had lunch at the same time, but we had to eat in groups. The first group would eat and leave, then the second group would eat. You could eat free by helping to cleanup the tables. Mr. Davis had a snack shop that was opened at lunch time.

Daisy Jackson Thomas
Class of 1950

WORKING

My late brother, Charles Carter, liked having money of his own. My parents could not provide same. He spoke to Mr. Ruffin about helping out at school. Mr. Ruffin gave him a job making fires in the morning so that the rooms would be warm for the students when they arrived. He had to walk four miles each way. Sometimes it would be dark when he left home and dark when he returned. After the fires had been made in each classroom, he attended his classes. He once told me he was accosted by four White youths riding in a car. They thought that they would have some fun at his expense. He had a different thought. He ran into the woods and hid. They did not find him. After they left, he walked home. I think the year that Charles graduated was 1943.

Dorothy Carter Black
Class of 1952

My father was a farmer. He gave my sister [Naomi Miller Woolfolk] and me one-half acres of tomatoes to tend. After we harvested the crop, he would take us to the tomato factory in SignBoard (where Signboard Road is located now) to sell our crop. He had us open a checking account at Union Bank and Trust. After we sold our crop, we would deposit the money in our checking account. When it was time to purchase our text books, we would write a check to pay for them.

Yvonne Woolfolk Britton
Class of 1947

I did not participate in many clubs at school because I was working. My grandfather [Lewis T. Washington] owned two places of business. One was the Cosmopolitan Inn in Guinea. The other was the Villeberro Inn in Woodford. They were a combination store, restaurant, and dance hall. From the time I was 5 or 6 until 1950, I used to like to stick around my grandfather. To me it was fun; I did not realize I was working.

Jesse Jackson
Class of 1947

I worked on the family farm when I was in school. I had to milk the cows every day before I went to school. Monday was wash day, so I would get up around 5 or 5:30 a.m., milk the cows, do the wash, and hang the clothes on the line before I went to school. When I came home from school, I would milk the cows, do my chores, eat, do my homework, and go to bed. During the summer, I worked in the fields [of the family farm] and harvested the crops in the fall.

Shirley Johnson Twiggs
Class of 1949

My parents had 10 children. We were expected to work in the summer to raise money for school. We picked tomatoes and cucumbers and canned vegetables. One summer, we picked 86 bushels of cucumbers in one day. We would take the cucumbers to a pickle factory in Milford and the tomatoes to a tomato factory in SignBoard, Penola, and sell them. We would break and bag sumac and sell it to a dye factory in Milford near the pickle factory. The factory used the sumac to make dye, and they paid for it by the pound. We would kill hogs and sell them.

Jeanetta Rock Lee
Class of 1952
Secretary

I was the janitor at the USO building. I would go there in the morning before school and in the evening after school. In the 12th grade, I worked on a poultry farm. I went to work from 7 until 8 in the morning, would go home, and then go to school. After school, I would work on the farm for about 2 hours and go home. I did that 5 days a week. On Saturdays, I worked from 8 a.m. until 12 noon. I brought a '39 Ford and a '47 Chevy convertible. I drove to school and would park at Josie Redd's. I also had a motorbike.

Morton Upshaw
Class of 1953

The summer after I completed the 11th grade, I went to New York to work. I did not come back to Caroline County for a whole year. When the job ended, my friends and parents told me I should finish school. I went back to school in the Fall of 1961 and graduated in 1962.

Waverly Minor
Class of 1962

I worked a lot when I was in school. I worked on other people's farms. In the fall, I started school a week late every year because I was working on the farm, cutting corn and soybeans. I also worked on the farm after school and on Saturdays. I worked about an hour. In the winter, I would feed the cows. In the spring, I would plant soybeans and corn. I would harvest in the Fall. I would get home around 6:30–7 p.m. I did most of my homework during study hall at school.

Rev. Joseph Dobbins
Class of 1959

In the 9th grade, I worked in the summer. I cleaned houses, washed clothes, and sat with the elderly. I gave some of the money to my mother. I also used some of the money to buy school supplies. I did not work during the school year.

Beulah Collins
Class of 1959

I had several jobs while I was a student. I worked in W. T. Grant Five and Dime store in Fredericksburg, Virginia, in the summer and after school. I worked at Quantico. My senior year, I worked for a plant that made picture frames. I worked from 4 p.m. to 12 a.m. I helped my parents pay to send my brother to college.

Calvin B. Taylor Sr.
Class of 1969

My siblings and I worked on a neighbor's farm in the summer to earn money for school clothes and supplies. We picked tomatoes, 10 cents a basket. I could go with the boys. The goal was to make 10 dollars on a good day. If you made 5 dollars a day you were doing good. We also sucked tobacco and shucked corn. But the big thing was picking tomatoes. We would get paid cash at the end of the day. We would take the money home and give it to our mother to save. At the end of the summer, she would give it back to us. We would catch the Trailways bus to Richmond to shop for school clothes. That was a big day. We did not have to buy our books because they were handed down from our older cousins.

Joyce Woolfolk Spencer
Attended Union High 1967–1969
Graduated from Bowling Green Senior High School 1971

ENROLLMENT

I was born in Washington, D.C., and attended school there through the 11th grade (Charles Young Elementary, Brown Junior High, and Spingarn High School). My father [Burley Brown] was from Caroline County. I would go to Caroline County every summer to stay with my grandmother [Emma Jane Turner]. In 1955, my grandmother needed someone to help her, so when I went to visit that summer, I stayed and went to Union High in the fall.

There was a big difference between Spingarn and Union. The building and class size were much smaller at Union. I had enough credits to graduate coming from D.C. because Spingarn offered more classes. I did not have problems adjusting because I knew some people from the neighborhood, Gloria Woodfolk and her sister, Alice. Also, I knew people because my grandmother was very well-known in the community.

Joyce "Judy" Brown Crump
Class of 1957

Ida Baylor Paige (l) and her daughter Gladys Paige (r) at 1932 graduation. COURTESY MARGUERITE DAVIS JACKSON.

My grandmother, Ida Baylor Paige, got married at a very early age and had four children. She returned to Union High in the 1930s and graduated with her daughter, Gladys Paige, in 1932. When she was in her mid-70s, she decided she wanted to become a nurse. She took a nursing correspondence course and after passing the exam worked as a nurse for approximately four years.

Kenneth Paige
Grandson of Ida Paige

I was born in Washington, D.C. My parents were from Caroline County. I would go back and forth between Washington, D.C., and staying with my grandmother [Martha Ferguson Galloway Baylor] in Caroline County. I started high school in Washington, D.C., at Phelps. I went back to Caroline County in the 12th grade and went to Union.

Charles Woodfork
Class of 1950

Mrs. Fanny Saunders Garnett was 15 years old in 1948 when she left Union High in the 10th grade. She married William Garnett, and together they had 12 children. Several of her children attended Union High and were taught by some of the same teachers Mrs. Garnett had when she was a student. One of those

teachers was Mrs. Dungee, who had taught Mrs. Garnett when she was in the tenth grade.

In 1977, the Caroline County School system began to offer adult education classes. Mrs. Dungee told Mrs. Garnett about the program and encouraged her to enroll. Mrs. Garnett enrolled and began taking classes in the evening in preparation for taking the General Educational Development (GED) exam. Mrs. Dungee was her social studies and English teacher. Mrs. Dungee described Mrs. Garnett as a good student who was determined to pass the GED exam on the first try (something that not too many students did). Mrs. Garnett received her high school diploma in the spring of 1979 after passing the GED exam on her first attempt.

FROM A FREE LANCE STAR ARTICLE[53]

I was born in Pennsylvania. My mother was from Caroline County. When I was about 2 years old, we moved back to Caroline County and stayed until the 1940s. I started school at Union elementary and went there grades 1–3. At first, I had to ride the high school bus to get to school. I

(l. to r.) Front row: Fanny Saunders Garnett, husband William Sr. and children: Carolyn, Sharon and Robert; second row: Rhonda, James, Kathleen, David, Shelia, Roderick and Crystal. Children not pictured: William Jr. and Leon D. Garnett. COURTESY FREE LANCE STAR, APRIL 24, 1979.

would sit on the older student's laps because the bus was full. My mother had a cousin, Eleanor Lucas, who lived near Union. I went to stay with her during the school year and could walk to school. After the 3rd grade, we moved, and I went to St. James school for grades 4 through 6. I could walk to school. When I finished the 6th grade, my family moved back to Pennsylvania. I went to grades 7 through 9 in Pennsylvania.

We moved back to Caroline County after I finished the 9th grade. The staff at Union High did not know what to do with me because I was suppose to be in the 10th grade and there was no 10th grade. The school had just added the 12th grade. They thought about putting me in the 9th grade, but since I had been an honor student they decided to put me in the 11th grade. I did not have any problem adjusting and continued to be an honor student.

*Cassandra Marie Davis
Brown
Class of 1950*

I started Union elementary in 1936 and left Union High in 1947 when I was in the 10th grade to join the military. I joined the Air Force when I was 17 years old. I went to several schools while I was in the military. Many years later, I decided I wanted to finish high school. I contacted Mr. Ruffin and told him I wanted to finish school. He wrote a letter to the military. I received my GED through the military in 1962. I retired from the Air Force October 1, 1967, after completing over 20 years of service with duties in Germany, Greenland, Canada, Africa, and many places in the United States, retiring in Wichita, Kansas.

*Oliver Latney Jr.
Attended Union High in the 1940s*

SEGREGATION

At the time, attending a segregated school did not bother me because that is all I knew. We were friends with the White children in our community. We would go to each other's houses to play, and our families helped each other. We did not encounter much discrimination because our parents taught us to avoid the situations (eg., segregated movies, restaurants, etc.). About once a month, my mother would take us to Richmond on the Trailways bus to shop and visit the hairdresser. We would go to a restaurant on 2nd Street in Jackson Ward (where the Black businesses were located). This was a treat.

*Yvonne Woolfolk Britton
Class of 1947*

I felt segregation was wrong when I was going to school, and it was a disadvantage. I

Oliver Latney Jr., 1955, Geiger Air Force Base, Spokane, Washington. COURTESY OLIVER LATNEY JR.

wanted to be a doctor. The only way I could go to college was on a state scholarship to a state school. There was not a Black college or university in Virginia that offered the medical courses that I wanted to take. I was the fourth of nine children in my family, the first to go to college. If I had graduated from an integrated high school, I could have gone to the University of Virginia. They had the classes that I wanted. It was not until 1954 that Brown v. The Board of Education decision stated Blacks were allowed to enter any college or university that they wished to attend. That victory did away with separate but equal schools.

Union High was separate but far from equal to Caroline or Ladysmith high schools (the two White high schools in the county).

*Daisy Jackson Thomas
Class of 1950*

I graduated from high school four years before Brown v. the Board of Education, and at that time, there was little if any discussion at Union High of segregated schools. It was a fact of life, and I certainly in no way felt that I was in a deprived setting.

Emma Samuel Vaughan
Class of 1950

Attending a segregated school did not bother me. The facility may have been separate and not equal, but we did not let that prevent us from getting our education. We had everything we needed even though we were probably considered to be poor. We had goals, and we set out to accomplish them. Segregation did not bother us because we knew who we were, where we were going, and what we needed to do to get there.

Jeanetta Rock Lee
Class of 1952
Secretary

I don't remember any open racism. People just kept to themselves. My parents' attitude toward segregation was "If they [White people] don't want us around, we will patronize our own businesses." My parents thought Union High was the best school for me. We may not have had the best supplies as the Whites, but it was made up for by the genuine concern of the teachers.

Calvin Taylor Sr.
Class of 1969

I did not think twice about attending a segregated school at the time. In retrospect, I see it was good for us at the time. The teachers had a vested interest in us. They went above and beyond. They encouraged us and cared about us. We had parents at home and parents at school.

Eleanor Thomas Hawkins
Class of 1965

I did not feel it [segregation] was a problem then. [At Union High] we got a good education and were loved. I did not have any problems. The [White] man's farm I worked on in the summer had a daughter. I would have friendly conversations with her. He treated us nicely and would give us lunch and a cool drink.

Joyce Woolfolk Spencer
Attended Union High 1967–1969
Graduated from Bowling Green Senior High
School 1971

CLASS PICTURES

11th Grade 1930–1931 (l. to r.). First row: unknown, unknown, unknown; second row: unknown, unknown, Stanley Jones; third row: unknown, unknown, Thomas Jones; back row: Addison Smith, James Pleasant, Davis Latney, Lynn Jones. COURTESY THE ARCHIE G. RICHARDSON PAPERS, ACCESSION #1997-77, SPECIAL COLLECTIONS AND ARCHIVES, JOHNSTON MEMORIAL LIBRARY, VIRGINIA STATE UNIVERSITY, PETERSBURG, VIRGINIA.

Union High Class of 1935, (l. to r.) front row: Mildred Beverly, unknown, Beatrice Redd, unknown, unknown; second row: unknown, Dorothy Saunders, Josephine Beverly; back row: unknown, unknown. COURTESY THE ARCHIE G. RICHARDSON PAPERS, ACCESSION #1997-77, SPECIAL COLLECTIONS AND ARCHIVES, JOHNSTON MEMORIAL LIBRARY, VIRGINIA STATE UNIVERSITY, PETERSBURG, VIRGINIA.

Union High Class of 1937, (l. to r.) James Freeman, Spurgeon Young, Edith Fraulein Coleman, Edward Ragland, Margaret Samuels, Helen Parker, Ruby King, Viola Miller, Walker Norman, Thelma Byrd, Vincent Coleman, Ulman Byrd. COURTESY VERGIE L. MILLER.

Union High Class of 1938, (l. to r.) first row: Ernestine Parker, Lou Banks, Viola Dudley, Vergie Miller, Thomas Hardman, Sarah Jeter, Sadie Johnson, Evelyn Wright; second row: Lula Young, Madge Richard, Jessie Warfield, Edward Wright, Annie Williams, Alberta Wright, Mary Jeter; third row: Mrs. Virginia Scott Jackson   Not pictured Lloyd Boxley and Elijah King. COURTESY VERGIE L. MILLER.

Union High Class of 1939, (l. to r.) front row: unknown, Bernice Scott, unknown Baker, unknown Baker, Louise Taylor, Catherine Childs, Edith Terrell; second row: Mary Edwards, Hattie Turner, Delia Gray, Victoria Scott, unknown; third row: unknown, unknown, Charles Ragland, Virginia Scott Jackson (teacher). COURTESY WESLEY T. CARTER.

Union High Class of 1941, (l. to r.), first row: Warren P. Hill, Lucille Golden, Thelma Johnson, Juanita U. Baker, Oddessa L. Coleman, Gladys P. Rich, Gladys A. Washington, Mary Louise Reeves; second row: Ethel L. Scott, Marion C. Bryant, Clarissa V. Galloway, Clars B. Moore, Gladys I. Bates, Aurelia M. Courtney, Sarah Fells, Magnolia E. Gregory; third row: Corine B. Baylor, Earline P. Baylor, Lucy Johnson, Daisy I. Purce, Lucille Peatross, Henrietta Davis, Lucille Jones, Mabel A. Dudley, Eloise E. Upshaw, Georgie Anna Upshaw, Catherine E. Taylor, Adolphus E. Johnson, Louis W. Keys; fourth row: Ernest G. Fife, Philip N. Roye, Parish D. Freeman, Julius R. Latney, George B. Ruffin (principal), Virginia Scott Jackson (teacher), Pitman G. Rock, Everett H. Byrd, William H. Smith, Arthur L. Coleman, Elmore Johnson Jr. COURTESY GLADYS RICH FERGUSON.

Union High Class of 1942 Top row: Garnett Jones, Ella Frye, Robert Miller, Josephine Turner, Edith Washington. Simon Alsop. Geraldine Frye and Lucille Johnson. Second row: Madeline Beverly, Ruth Shepherd, Cecil Craighead, Blanche Rich, Bernice Banks, Archie Grey, Ruth Golden and Lucy Johnson. Third row: Thelma Derricott, Melvin Byrd, George B. Ruffin (Principal), Virginia Jackson (teacher), Cosmore Coleman and Elizabeth Thomas. Fourth row: Virgie Frye, Stanley Hill, Bessie Taylor, Fannie Anderson, Maggie Washington, Bud Taylor and Martha Frye. Bottom row: Susie Garnett, Bernard Johnson, Juanita Williams, Percy Baylor, Randolph Derricott, Mary Washington and Elizabeth Turner. COURTESY FREE LANCE STAR, FEBRUARY 24, 1996.

Union High Class of 1943. COURTESY ERCELLE DEYO BYRD.

Union High Class of 1945. COURTESY JANIE ANDERSON EDWARDS

Union High Class of 1947, (l. to r.) front row: Susie Carter, Sarah Latney, Arlene Burruss, Laverne Baylor, Alma Thomas, Blanche Courtney, Daisy Harrison, Linda Christopher, Mildred Childs, Doris Latney; second row: Evelyn Burruss, Laverne Fortune, Geneva Samuels, Geneva Coats, Irene Quash, Gladys Beverly, Mary King; third row: Catherine Gregory, Rubie Byrd, Lenora Fells, Yvonne Woolfolk, Albania J. Johnson, Mary Moore, Fannie Bundy, Dorothy Wilson, Marion Johnson, Mariam Fortune; fourth row: Granville Lewis, Joseph Twiggs, Pearl Pleasant, Thelma Washington, Evelyn Fields, Audrey Moore, Wilhelmina Garnett, Pearl Upshaw, Bessie Lewis, George Monroe, Frank Johnson, Mary Boxley; back row: Ernest Freeman, Jessie Jackson, Harry Fells, Smith Young, Williard Shepherd, Robert Alsop. COURTESY YVONNE WOOLFOLK BRITTON.

Union High Class of 1948. COURTESY WALTER YOUNG.

Union High Class of 1952. COURTESY MARGUERITE DAVIS JACKSON.

Union High Class of 1955. COURTESY CAROLINE PROGRESS, MARCH 12, 2009.

Union High Class of 1958, COURTESY BEULAH COLLINS.

Union High Class of 1959, COURTESY MARGUERITE DAVIS JACKSON.

Union High
Class of 1962
SOURCE: 1962 UNION
HIGH YEARBOOK.

Union High
Class of 1966
COURTESY CAROLYN
BUNDY JOHNSON.

Facilities

In the early years, the Union High facilities were wood-frame buildings that had been built in the 1920s. Electricity was later added, but the buildings were poorly lit. The facilities lacked indoor plumbing and were heated by

Old Buildings. SOURCE: UNION HIGH 50TH ANNIVERSARY PROGRAM

pot belly stoves or wood burned in tin barrels. The cafeteria was small and inadequate, so many students ate their lunches in their homerooms.

In the 1940s, the school board made several additions and improvements to the Union High campus. A shop building was constructed with funds from the National Youth Administration.[54] The $8,000 from the sale of Negro schools to the U.S. government during the acquisition of land to establish AP Hill was used to install a drinking water supply and build a home economics cottage. Benches from the Mica School auditorium (a White high school) where removed and installed at Union High.[55] Four temporary classrooms were constructed for the elementary grades.[56] A building was purchased from the Essex County school system and moved to Union High.[57] The trustee board and the Sunday School Union also gave funds to have a portion of the basement converted to a lunchroom.

By the mid 1940s, the Union High buildings had become worn, outdated, and overcrowded. Most schools in the Caroline County school system were in same state of disrepair. In a January 26, 1946, Free Lance Star newspaper article, Mr. W. A. Vaughn, division superintendent of schools, described the schools:

"They are physically unattractive, are uncomfortable due to poor construction and design and method of heating and ventilation, and do not conform to the approved conditions as to sanitation.

"It is almost a farce to attempt to teach health and sanitation in such a school environment. On very cold days, pupils spend a good part of the day hovering around the stove to keep warm. It is impossible to maintain a temperature throughout a school room heated by a stove. Rooms frequently become overheated."[58]

On May 6, 1945, the school board adopted a resolution to establish a long-term improvement plan that called for upgrading some schools and consolidating smaller schools into newly constructed facilities. The plan also included a new facility for Union High School.[59] The 1950–1951 school board budget included plans to construct a $300,000 facility for Union High School that would consist of a separate auditorium and gymnasium, cafeteria, science laboratories, home economics departments, shop, administrative offices, and classrooms.[60]

After reviewing the bids for the construction project, the school board realized the new school would cost more than expected. The board met with members of the Countywide League and presented several options for keeping the cost down, one of which was to combine the gymnasium and the auditorium. The members of the Countywide League did not agree with the suggestion and submitted a letter to the school board requesting that a separate auditorium and gymnasium and a cafeteria be kept in the plan.[61] Their request was granted. Construction began on the new facility in March 1951 and was completed in 1952.

In January of 1952, the high school grades moved to the new modern brick building. The primary grades were taught in the old USO building, and grades 6 and 7 were taught in the old Union High buildings. A new elementary school was built in 1959.

Three additions were made to the Union High building to accommodate the ever-increasing student population. In 1956, a band room, an audio-visual aids room, and four addition classrooms were added; five classrooms were added in 1961; and another four classrooms were added in 1964.[62]

While the school board financed the construction of the facility and the additions, the Sunday School Union, administration, and members of the community worked hard to raise funds to install shrubbery, draperies, and other accessories to enhance and beautify the school. When Union High ceased to exist in 1969, the facility was the largest and most modern high school in the Caroline County school system.

There were three buildings. One was a two-story building. There were four rooms on the first floor: one for the elementary grades 1–3, one for the elementary grades 4–7, a science lab, and a home economics room. The second floor contained the library and three rooms for high school. The principal's office was at the end of the front hall on the second floor. The stairway in the front was for the girls; the stairway in the back was for the boys.

A second building contained the auditorium-chapel on the first floor and dormitories on the top floor. A cafeteria was built in the basement in the later years. The third building was the agricultural-shop building. Mr. Davis had a snack shop, called the Pie Shop, where students could buy snacks at lunchtime.

The buildings had electricity but no indoor plumbing. They were heated by burning wood in an oil-drum stove. Students had to bring wood in from outside. We did not have to chop it, just bring it in. The floors were wooden; they put oil on the floors to keep them clean. There was a baseball field outside.

Lillian Richardson Sizer
Class of 1946

A big bell was on the top of the school with a rope that hung down inside the school. [A student would] pull the rope and ring the bell when classes started and when it was time to change classes and also when it was time to dismiss for the day.

Clara Latney Hudson
Class of 1949

My father [George Davis] had a snack stand where he would sell items during lunchtime. It was between the chapel and the academic building. The students called it the Window. They would say, "Are you going to the Window?" My parents [George Davis and Laly Golden Davis] would stand inside, and the students would come up to the window and purchase items. RC Cola was a very popular item—it was 5 cents.

Marguerite Davis Jackson
Class of 1945
English Teacher
Guidance Counselor

Classroom building (left) and snack stand (right). Source: 1945 *Union High Yearbook.*

The school was a wood-frame building. The steps were very squeaky. They would ring the bell when it was time for the students to come inside. Mr. Ruffin would say, "Don't ring the bell too hard. It might fall down." The building had electricity but no indoor plumbing. There were barrel heaters in each classroom.

> *Susie Carter Quash*
> *Class of 1947*

We were very appreciative of the new building. It had indoor plumbing, better and modern science and home economics equipment. The students were very excited.

> *Vivian Garnett Coleman*
> *Class of 1953*

I started high school in the old building. There were two wooden buildings. The elementary grades, chapel-auditorium were in one building. The high school was in the other building. It has two floors. You would take more than one class in the same classroom. You would take a class in one subject in the classroom and come back to the same classroom in the afternoon for another subject. We did not have a gym. We used to play outside in the dirt. For gym class, we had to climb a rope to the 2nd floor. We played basketball and baseball outside. The building had electricity, but it did not have indoor plumbing. Mr. Davis had a little building where we would buy snacks at lunchtime. Coconut pie was 10 cents, and soda was 7 cents. You would get 2 cents back when you returned the bottle.

It was like a dream come true when we moved to the new building. Everything was new and modern. It was next to the USO building. A lot of the items were donated by the Sunday School Union. There was indoor plumbing. The library had new books. Students each had their own lockers in the hallway. There was a gym with bleachers and locker rooms with showers, one for the girls and one for boys. There was a classroom for each subject. There was a PA system in the principal's office. There was a new cafeteria with a kitchen where they cooked meals.

> *Charles Gray*
> *Class of 1952*

I went to the 8th grade in the old building. It was very old and almost falling down. The floor was warped in some places. The next year, we moved to the new building. The students helped move items to the new building. The boys from the baseball team helped move the furniture. The school board had some people supervising.

Everyone was very happy when we moved into the new building. Everything was new. We could not believe we had such a nice new building. It was brand new and had indoor plumbing. It had a gym with nice wood floors, bleachers, showers, and locker rooms. In the old building, the boys played basketball outside in the dirt.

The classrooms were modern, and there were new desks in every classroom. Each student had their own locker. The home ec room was like a little apartment. It had a stove, dining room, living room, and new sewing machines. There were separate rooms for sewing and cooking. In the old building, everything was in the same room.

The cafeteria was large. You went down a serving line with stainless steel counters to get your food. There was a kitchen were they cooked all the food. There was a huge auditorium were we had assemblies every Friday. Mr. Ruffin and the teachers instilled into the students to have pride in the new building and to take care of it. The building was nicer than the White high school. The students took pride in the building. Most of the students tried to take care of it.

Anonymous
Class of 1956

The Virginia Teachers Association had experience working with various school systems in Virginia who were building new schools. When the new building was being built, they advised the Union High administration to get the gymnasium, cafeteria, and auditorium when the school was first built because it would be easier to get additional classrooms later. We were told if we did not get a separate gymnasium, cafeteria, and auditorium in the original building, we would never get it. The county was required to build more classrooms because they were responsible for educating the students. Several additions were made to the school after it was built.

Dr. Walter E. Lowe
Industrial Arts Teacher
Assistant Principal

Opposite: The New Union High School before annex. Source: Marguerite Davis Jackson.

(This page, clockwise from top right)
Office • Cafeteria • Industrial Arts Shop
• Home Economics Department, Kitchen
• Home Economics Department, Dining
Room • Home Economics Department,
Living Room • Auditorium

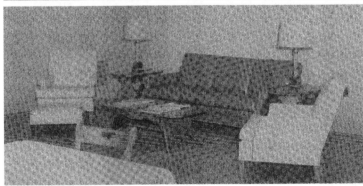

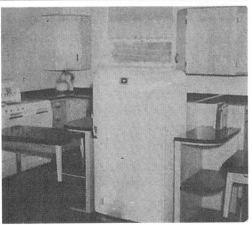

(Top) Classroom; (bottom) Library

Curriculum

The curriculum at Union High consisted of both academic and vocational courses. A review of the Aims and Objectives of the Various Departments of Union High School shows that in addition to teaching a subject, the teachers were interested in improving the students in all aspects of their lives. They also wanted to:

> develop skills values, attitudes, and high moral standards which will make our children well-rounded citizens of this country, this state, this nation, and this world[63]

> develop in each pupil the habit of self-reliance, self-discipline, and resourcefulness in meeting practical situations[64]

> develop in each pupil a feeling of pride in his ability to do useful things and to develop worthwhile leisure time activities[65]

> develop in each pupil a readiness to assist others and to join happily in group undertakings[66]

> to provide experiences for the students which will help them to develop initiative, accuracy, alertness, leadership, promptness, and responsibility[67]

Many Union High alumni felt the school did a good job of preparing them for life after high school, but some students believed the curriculum was not very robust. In the fall of 1963, the Union High Parent Teacher Association asked the Caroline County School Board to study the school's curriculum to see how it could be improved. The PTA was concerned because some of the school's graduates did not feel they were sufficiently prepared for college or given ample business or technical training to obtain employment after high school graduation.[68]

Of the students who felt they were not academically prepared for life after high school, most stated that despite the shortcomings of the Union High curriculum, the life skills they learned at home and school allowed them to rise to the challenge and take the necessary actions to become successful in life.

GENERAL

I took English (4 years), algebra, geometry, general science, biology, chemistry, history, government, French (2 years), and home economics. Supplies were limited, so we worked in groups. When the White school got new furniture, etc., Union High got their old items. We had to buy our books. My parents gave me the money for books. Home economics was one hour. We did cooking and sewing—Mrs. Banks taught both.

Lillian Richardson Sizer
Class of 1946

I took every class that was offered to girls. We needed 16 units to graduate. By the time I was a senior, I had accumulated 21 units. A lot of the classes were easy. The math was challenging, chemistry kept me on my toes. I do feel that the equipment that we had was not adequate for us. Classrooms did not have adequate supplies and equipment. Rooms did not have maps, globes, audio-visual equipment, and so on.

Daisy Jackson Thomas
Class of 1950

My favorite subjects were English and French, both taught by my favorite teacher and role model Mrs. Louis E. Carter. I regarded Mrs. Carter as the epitome of what a school teacher should be like: intelligent, articulate, interesting, and friendly. I especially enjoyed the literary selections we studied. Vicariously, I shared the romance, intrigue, and adventure in which the characters were involved. I read not only the assigned selections but as many of the others as I could understand. Our study of poetry included a concentrated study of versification. That was great fun. I did not particularly like the study of grammar, especially parsing sentences. Memorization and presentation of selected literary selections was a vital part of our study of literature. Because of our limited library resources, our literature assignments were almost exclusively from the textbook. By the time I started attending Union High, I had already memorized many of the regularly assigned literary selections. That heightened my interest in them. Most of our creative writing exercises involved responding to the literature we read.[69]

Florence Coleman Bryant
Class of 1940

French and English lit were taught by Mrs. T. T. Jackson. English was my favorite subject. We had to memorize a number of poems. Among them were "The Rainy Day" by Henry Wadsworth Longfellow, "Daffodils" by William Wordsworth, "The Last Leaf" by Oliver Wendell Holmes, and the last verse of "Thanatopsis" by William Bryant. I never lost my love for English lit, and at 50 years of age (1984) I began studies at the George Washington University, receiving a Bachelor of Arts degree in Education and Human Development in 1989.

Dorothy Samuels Jackson
Class of 1950

I felt Union High did the best they could, but the curriculum was not as robust. There was not much variety in subject matter. They did a good job of preparing us for life in general.

Evelyn Wright Thompson
Class of 1958

I was allowed to make additions to the curriculum. I just had to justify the addition. I created a jazz band. I developed a feeder system for the Union High band by starting a music program at the elementary school next door [Union Elementary] for the 5th and 6th graders. Mr. Guss [principal of Union Elementary] was very supportive. The new band director [Richard Burnett] continued the program after I left Union High.

Blonnie Tipton
Band Teacher

Drivers education was nothing like today. Before we could get behind the steering wheel of a car to drive, we were required to learn the major parts of a car and how each part functioned. Once we passed this portion of the driver education process, we were then allowed to get behind the steering wheel of the car and actually drive. At the completion of both parts of the class, we then received our learner's permit from the area state police.

Cassandra Marie Davis Brown
Class of 1950

In the early years, the curriculum was not as complete as the faculty wanted it to be. The curriculum did not have the variety of courses we would have liked. There were a group of educators who would go to the school board and advocate for new classes. The curriculum got stronger in the later years because the school board was more willing to provide a variety of courses.

Walter Lowe
Industrial Arts Teacher
Coach
Assistant Principal

AGRICULTURAL

The goal of the agricultural class was to teach students the basics of animal and plant science, farm mechanics and management, farm family living, and leadership training. Instructional services were also provided at the Community Cannery, farm machinery repair, and adult evening classes. Instructors also served as agricultural consultants to members of the community.

Mr. Banks demonstrates the proper procedure for cutting pork chops. SOURCE: *1956 UNION HIGH YEARBOOK.*

Mr. Boxley's students test the acidity of soil.
SOURCE: *1956 UNION HIGH YEARBOOK.*

BUSINESS EDUCATION

SOURCE: *1959 UNION HIGH YEARBOOK.*

The first business classes, typing and shorthand (called commercial science), were added to the curriculum in 1949. The business curriculum went by a variety of names over the years: commercial science, commerce, and business education. It was expanded to include stenography, bookkeeping, clerical practice. The goal of business education was two-fold: to provide all students with basic business, bookkeeping, and personal use typewriting skills and to provide students interested in clerical careers with typing, bookkeeping, and stenography skills, as well as work experience.

Business education was introduced to Union High in 1949. As seniors, we were allowed to take typing (on new typewriters) and shorthand. That was the first new equipment I had seen in the school. We were excited.
Daisy Jackson Thomas
Class of 1950

ENGLISH

The goal of the English department was to help students develop oral and written expression, reading, literature, handwriting, and spelling.

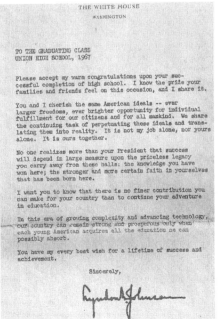

The students in the English IV class a wrote to President Lyndon B. Johnson. This is a copy of the letter they received in response. SOURCE: *THE POINTER REVIEW, JUNE 1967.*

FOREIGN LANGUAGE

Latin was taught in the 1930s In the 1940s, the language was changed to French, and the curriculum was designed to provide students basic language skills in listening, speaking, reading, and writing.

Our French studies involved primarily studying grammar, memorizing dialog, and translating excerpts from literature. I tried to imitate Mrs. Carter's pronunciations and intonation as precisely as I could. Sometimes I took my French textbook to the outhouse at home and had the time of my life reading and listening to my own voice quality. As was typical of language instruction during that time, we concentrated very little on conversational language. I continued my interest in the study of French in college, taking all of the courses offered there. In fact, French became one of my minors at Virginia State College.[70]

Florence Coleman Bryant
Class of 1940

We would have French week in French class. During this time, we would be required to speak only French.

William Brawner
Class of 1966

HEALTH AND PHYSICAL EDUCATION

The health and physical education curriculum was intended to teach students about hygiene and body functions and how to develop a healthy lifestyle by exercising and participating in sports.

Our physical education and health classes were the most neglected of all our classes. Conducted by a homeroom teacher, the physical education activities were done outside during the fall and spring, and the health lessons were done indoors during the winter and inclement weather. We had no ath-

letic equipment, so there was very little variety in the program. The athletically inclined students dominated the outdoor sports, baseball, softball, volleyball, and basketball. I was more of a passive player because I was not very good at sports.[71]

Florence Coleman Bryant
Class of 1940

HOME ECONOMICS

Home economics was added to the curriculum part time during the 1935–1936 school year. A home economics teacher was hired to teach one 90-minute home economics period a day and other subjects the remainder of the day. The class consisted of 60 girls and a limited amount of equipment: an old range; a few heavy white mugs; a lard tin; one dish pan; a few knives, forks and spoons; and two very old sewing machines.[72]

A full-time accredited vocational home economics program was added to the curriculum during the 1936–1937 school year.[73] In the early years, it included units in cooking, sewing, home care, interior decoration, and personal development. Over the years, the curriculum was expanded to include child care and development, money management, health and home nursing, preparation for marriage, family living, food and nutrition, and leadership training.

We had a sewing project in home economics. When I took my project home, my mother, who was a beautiful seamstress, said, "You are not going to turn that in." She made me take it apart and sew it again. I never told Mrs. Banks what happened.

Emma Samuel Vaughan
Class of 1950

We had to do home economics projects over the summer—canning, gardening, etc. The home economics teacher would come to our home to check on the status of our project.

Kate Hutchison Samuels
Class of 1950

Home economics prepared me for life. I learned planning and caring for a family, sewing, saving money, and interior decorating.

Aterita Baker Brown
Attended Union High from 1958 to1961

Mrs. Banks and Mrs. Ragland were the home economics teachers. One taught cooking, and the other taught sewing. I don't remember which one taught which. I was not good at sewing—it took me two weeks to make a skirt. The hardest part was the zipper. I don't think I ever got that right. The cooking part was not that bad. I was the oldest girl at home, so I cooked at home.

Florence Lee Rhue
Class 1965

Home economics was one of the most valuable courses I took at Union High School. Unfortunately, I did not perform to my satisfaction in the course. My problem was that the class was very large, so we had to work in groups to complete the units of study. It was impossible for the teacher to give each student the individual attention necessary to ensure mastery of the concepts covered by the individual units. Working as a member of a group, I was able to bluff my way through the parts of the course I did not like. For example, I hated cooking because I had had no experience doing it. At home, Mama did all of the cooking. When our group did the cooking unit, I volunteered to assemble the equipment and to do the cleanups. In sewing, I simply could not learn how to operate a treadle machine. My girlfriend was expert at sewing. She did my entire machine stitching, while I did the handwork. Between the two of us, I completed the unit satisfactorily. I enjoyed the units on home care and interior decoration and on personal development. For the interior decoration unit, we did a scrapbook illustrating our dream houses. It was fun to fantasize how I wanted my dream house to look and to clip and paste the beautiful room designs from magazines.

My home projects were something else. Mrs. Mary B. Banks, our home economics teacher, re-quired each student to select a project to complete at home, and we were supposed to keep a log of all of our activities pertaining to our home project. Mrs. Banks made home visits to her students' homes to evaluate their progress on their projects.

(l. to r.) Betty Johnson, Matilda Ferguson, Geraldine Terrell, Eleanor Thomas. Courtesy Pauline Shelton Boxley.

My home project was supposed to be to redecorate my bedroom. In the first place, I did not have a bedroom I could call my own. Myrtle, Esther, and I shared the same bedroom. In the second place, I had no time to do special projects at home. By the time I had completed my chores and my homework assignments, there was no time left for anything else. When Mrs. Banks came to my home to evaluate my project, which was beautiful on paper but was actually nonexistent, I felt anxious and nervous. I was supposed to be her hostess, but as soon as she and Mama became engaged in conversation, I disappeared and remained out of sight until Mrs. Banks had left. Mrs. Banks well understood the lifestyle and conditions of the farm, so I suspect she guessed that my project was more fantasy than fact. She explained her program to Mama, and they had a warm exchange, but she did not get to see my project, nor did she reprimand me about it.[74]

Florence Coleman Bryant
Class of 1940

Matilda Ferguson, Eleanor Thomas, Bertha Johnson, and Geraldine Terrell planned a mock wedding as part of the marriage unit in the cooking section of home economics. Mrs. Banks taught us how to plan and set up a wedding and wedding reception. We baked a wedding cake, made hors d'oeuvres, and had punch. Roger Mickens and Frances Smith were the big couple at the school. We picked them to be the bride and groom. We also picked girls from the class to be the bridesmaids and friends of the groom to be the groomsmen. The students had to be doing well in school to participate. On the day of the mock wedding, Roger forgot and did not wear a necktie. His friend, Roy Johnson had on a suit. Roger kept asking Roy to let him wear his jacket and tie, but Roy said no. Roy ended up being the groom in the mock wedding. The wedding was held in the living room-dining room section of the home ec class and was attended by students in the class. A few years later, Roger and Francis got married for real. They are still married today had have two children.

Eleanor Thomas Hawkins
Class of 1965

Home economics, 1949, (l. to r.) Louise Morton, Shirley Johnson, Susie Rock. COURTESY SHIRLEY JOHNSON TWIGGS.

Home economics students work on their sewing projects. SOURCE: 1952 UNION HIGH YEARBOOK.

Home economic students, late 1940s. Home economics students were required to prepare and serve luncheons for various school functions while their instructors observed and critiqued them. Seated (l. to r.) Susie Rock (student), Joseph Johnson (farm agent), Lloyd Boxley (agricultural teacher), unknown, unknown, unknown, Nettie Saunders (cafeteria worker); standing (l. to r.) home economics students Lorraine Fleming, unknown, unknown, unknown, Bessie Alsop, Judith Jones, Gloria Jean Bennett, Beverly Jones, unknown. COURTESY PAULINE SHELTON BOXLEY.

INDUSTRIAL ARTS AND MASONRY

Industrial arts was added to the curriculum in 1939. Masonry was added in the 1960s. Industrial arts and masonry provided students with an understanding of the use of common tools and machines, as well as common construction types and repairs. The goal was to assist the students in becoming self-reliant, disciplined, and resourceful.

Industrial arts was taught in the 8th through 12th grades. The purpose of Industrial Arts was to expose students to the trade and let them determine if they had the ability to work in the field. The first class taken in the 8th grade was an exploratory class to see if the students liked industrial arts. If they liked it, they could take more advanced classes. Skills taught were carpentry, brick laying, and electrical wiring. In the old building, the classes were taught in a separate building. (The small brick building to left that is behind the Community Center was the Agricultural Shop building.) In the new building, it [the industrial arts classroom] was in the same building but set apart from the other classes so the noise would not disturb the other classes.

Students were not given home projects. In the summer if they worked in the industrial arts field, I would give them credit. After graduation, students who had taken industrial arts classes could get a job as an apprentice or helper in the industrial arts field. Ronald Johnson (basketball and baseball player) started helping me when he was in the 7th grade; he started out handing me tools. This helped him get familiar with the tools. Ronald continued to work for me after graduation and worked for me until I closed my business in 1969, when I moved to teach at Virginia State University. Ronald now owns a general contracting business.

Dr. Walter Lowe
Industrial Arts Teacher
Assistant Principal
Coach

I took shop from Mr. Lowe. I made a shoeshine box, lamp, and magazine rack that I still have today. I've carried them with me all over the United States and back to Virginia.

Charles Gray
Class of 1952

Mr. Lowe taught us how to use tools and do carpentry work. During the school year, I worked for him in the evenings after school and on Saturday. In the summer, I worked full time. We helped build homes. That is how I made money. I brought my first car, a Ford pickup truck. I still use what I learned today. I fix things around my house and help others in the community. I worked for Mr. Lowe one year after I graduated.

Elmer Johnson
Class of 1962

Industrial arts students. SOURCE: *1964 UNION HIGH YEARBOOK.*

MATHEMATICS

Algebra students. SOURCE: *1954 UNION HIGH YEARBOOK.*

The early mathematics curriculum consisted of general mathematics. Over the years, the curriculum expanded to include general mathematics, algebra I and II, geometry, trigonometry, college prep math (Calculus). Math studies were intended to provide all students with an understanding of logical thinking.

Mr. Luckie took the top students from his class to a math competition in Richmond. It was during the week. We had to take a timed math test. I won first place for the 8th grade. It was exciting for me because we were competing with schools from the city like Maggie Walker, Armstrong, Carver, and Peabody. When they called my name, I was in a state of shock. It was a big deal to me because I was from a country school and I won first place. I think the teachers from Walker and Armstrong were surprised, too, because a student from rural Bowling Green had won first place.

Williabel Jones Davis
Class of 1966

I participated in science and math competitions several times. They were held in the spring. We would compete against students from other schools like Maggie Walker, Armstrong, and Virginia Randolph. They [the teachers] would select one or two students to compete in each subject (for example, algebra, geometry, biology, chemistry). It was exciting to be selected to represent Union High. One year, I won 2nd place in the algebra competition. We had 20 algebra problems to solve. After we took the test, they would grade them and hold an assembly later that day to announce the winner. I received a certificate; I was very excited.

Sherrillyn Smith Silver
Class of 1965

MUSIC

Choral music was added to the curriculum in 1947. During the 1956–1957 school year, instrumental music was added.

Choir rehearses for a concert. SOURCE: *1956 UNION HIGH YEARBOOK.*

UNION EXCELS AT DISTRICT SCIENCE AND MATH MEET

On April 8, 1961, the Science and Math Conference of the Southern Region was held at Armstrong High School in Richmond, Virginia. Two of Union High School students excelled in mathematics and physics. Judith Fortune, an eight grader, won second place in general mathematics. Charlie Wright, a sophomore, won first place in physics with his demonstration of STEARN'S DUPLEX TELEGRAPH AND RADIO TRANSMITTER. He selected this project in less than five hours. All parts of this project were made by Charlie Wright except the ignition cords.

Charlie and Judith will journey to Norfolk division of Virginia State College on Aril 22, 1961, to compete with students from all parts of the state.

SOURCE: *UNION HERALD, APRIL 28, 1961*

STUDENTS PERFORM IN ALL STATE BAND ACTIVITY

Every year, the Music Conference of Virginia Teachers Association plans an All State Band activity which consists of participants from various schools in the state of Virginia. This year the band consisted of 130 players. For many years, the All State Band had been meeting for one day. This year it was fortunate to have had three days.

On April 9, 1961, four of our outstanding students namely Willie Jackson, Phillip Byrd, Calvin Childs, and James Johnson participated in this grand affair. Although these students realized the difficulties of performing the numbers played, their progress was not hindered.

Most musicians present at the occasion agreed that the program was very difficult but also agree that this was the best performance presented in quite some time.

The numbers on the program were: "William Tell Overture," "Meditation," "Stand By March," "Doxology," "Victory At Sea," "March of the Nobles," and "Hands Across the Sea."

SOURCE: *UNION HERALD, APRIL 28, 1961*

Mr. Lee demonstrates the proper way to dissect a frog.

SCIENCE

Over the years, the science curriculum was expanded from general science to include biology, chemistry, and physics.

We dissected a frog in science class. There were about 20 students in class. We worked in 2 or 3 groups and took turns dissecting the frog.

Gladys Rich Ferguson
Class of 1941

SOCIAL STUDIES

Over the years, the curriculum was expanded to include civics, American history, geography, and world history.

VOCATIONAL EDUCATION

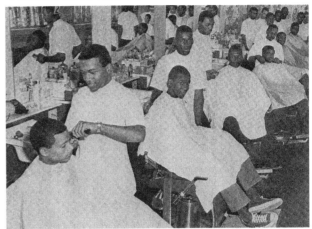

Barbering students. SOURCE: 1969 UNION HIGH YEARBOOK.

Commercial foods students. SOURCE: 1968 UNION HIGH YEARBOOK

Cosmetology students.
SOURCE: 1969 UNION HIGH YEARBOOK

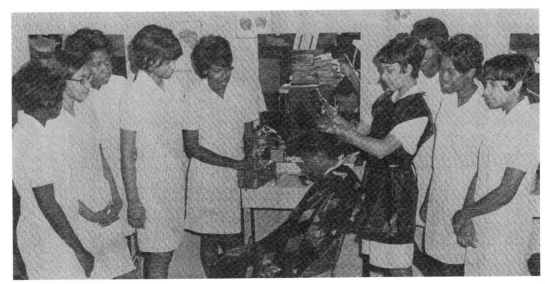

School Functions

Union High provided a variety of school functions. Assemblies (called chapel in the early years) were held throughout the school year. In the early years, chapel was held weekly, but later assemblies were less frequent. Programs included school announcements, guest speakers, talent shows, and campaigns for the student government officer positions. Functions were also held for special events such as Christmas, Thanksgiving, and Negro History Week.

Union High's proximity to Washington, D.C., and Richmond, Virginia, provided the opportunity for a range of field trips. For many students, this was their only occasion to leave the county.

May Day (called Field Day in the early years) was a source of entertainment for the entire community. Junior-senior prom allowed students to interact in a formal setting.

Baccalaureate and commencement was a major affair not just for Union High but for the entire community. Graduation from high school was seen as a significant accomplishment and was a source of great pride to the graduate's family and the community.

Other schools functions where the mother-daughter banquet, New Homemakers of America (NHA)-New Farmers of America (NFA) banquet, and homecoming.

ASSEMBLY-CHAPEL

Chapel was once a week. We had devotion and listened to announcements.
Lillian Richardson Sizer
Class of 1946

Charles Woodfork (drums), Colbert Freeman (guitar), Herbert Jackson (piano). Not pictured: Sparky Derricott (guitar). SOURCE: *1950 UNION HIGH YEARBOOK.*

We had assemblies once a week. It was good because it was the only time the whole school—teachers and students—came together. The chorus would sing. The principal and teachers would make speeches. The teachers would tell us about activities. We had school plays, and we performed at assembly.
Daisy Jackson Thomas
Class of 1950

We always had assemblies regularly. One day (it may have been my junior or senior year) during Negro History Week, a young lady from Fredericksburg spoke. I think her name was Jerine Mercer. I don't remember her exact words, but I know after that day, I felt good about being Black and proud of the things that Blacks had accomplished.

> *Patricia Sizer Adams*
> *Class of 1964*

We had a variety of assemblies: Negro History Week, entertainment from college choirs, the dramatic club, and talents shows. Students would come from other schools to perform as well.

> *Gladys Fitzhugh-Pemberton*
> *Class of 1964*

In February, we would have a program for Negro History Week. There would be speakers, and students would portray famous Black people. We would also have programs during Thanksgiving. Each class would prepare a Thanksgiving basket to distribute. The baskets would be on display during the assembly, and ministers from the community would speak.

> *Jeanetta Rock Lee*
> *Class of 1952*
> *Secretary*

A few students would sneak in the chapel when it was not in use and play the piano. One day, I brought my drum set to school, and a few students and I got together and began to play. Word got out that they were good, and people would ask us to play at their functions. We played at school functions and local clubs (Red Robin and the Oak Lodge) on Saturdays. We did not live near each other, so we didn't practice. We did not have cars, so we had to rely on friends for transporta-

tion. We did not get paid, we just played for fun. Although we were all Union High students, the band was not associated with the school.

> *Charles Woodfork*
> *Class of 1950*

I was friends with Vernelle Twiggs, Patsy Winston, and Carolyn Baylor. We called ourselves the Swinging Foxy Four. We would sometimes perform in talent shows together. We would meet at Vernelle's house to hang out. Vernelle introduced me to my husband, Pete Harris. At this 2010 year, we have been married for 40 years.

> *Regena Green Harris*
> *Class of 1967*

We had a fashion show every year around Easter. I was a page along with Fanny Saunders. We would skip down the aisle with a placard that showed the category for the clothes that were being modeled. We would go on the stage and hold our placards. One would stand on the right side, and the other, on the left side. The students would come down the aisle modeling their clothes in that category. After all the models finished that category, we would display placards for the next group.

I remember chapel on Fridays for devotions. The Lord's Prayer and Pledge of Allegiance were recited. We also sang songs such as "Onward Christian Soldiers," "America the Beautiful," "My Country 'Tis of Thee," and the "Negro National Anthem."

> *Dorothy Carter Black*
> *Class of 1952*

I was in a singing group called The School Girls. Other members of the group were Martha Lewis, Alice Wilson, and Ann Roye. We sang at talent shows and other assemblies at school. Our band

The Swinging Foxy Four at the 1967 junior-senior prom. (l. to r.) Regena Green, Vernelle Twiggs, Carolyn Baylor and Patsy Winston. COURTESY SHIRLEY JOHNSON TWIGGS.

teacher, Mr. Jennings, played bass in a professional band from Northern Virginia called the Courtney Brooks Orchestra. When the school had talent shows, the band would play for all the singing groups. Mr. Jennings and Mrs. Wilson [the music teacher] would rehearse us.

Clara Sizer Harris
Class of 1960

I was in a singing group called the Shellanies (Shel-lanies). Members were Gloria Hill (deceased), Sharon K. (Garnett) Allen, Vanessa (James) Ware, and Carolyn (Garnett) Epps. We had a dedicated manager, David Myers, who practiced with us at Maude's Grill in Bowling Green. He demanded that we work hard. We took pride in our ability to sing and the showmanship. We sang, danced, and entered on stage with grace, style, charm, sequenced steps, and coordinated outfits, just as the Supremes, Martha Reeves and the Vandellas, and others did. We stole the hearts of many and gained respect as one of the best female singing groups around (I believe we were the best). We sang at Union High's fashion and talent shows, as well as traveled to other local high schools.

I especially remembered the talent show at Walker T. Grant High School in Fredericksburg, Virginia. As we were introduced and walked out on the stage (with our black skirts, red sweaters, red socks, black shoes), you could see the packed auditorium, could feel the heat as if it were a 90 degree day, and silence as we approached the stage. The audience faces looked in anticipation and wonderment. Just as we began to sing and step to the "Shoop Shoop Song" ("It's in His Kiss") by Betty Everett, the crowd went mad. By the end of the performance, we had them standing in the seats, which told us that we had gained their respect. That was a golden and memorable night.

Carolyn Garnett Epps
Class of 1966

We had assemblies about once a month. There would be speakers; students would perform (play piano, sing, etc.). We would also have talent shows. Some assemblies were held to elect student government representatives. There would be nominations for different offices.

Evelyn Wright Thompson
Class of 1958

The School Girls perform at a talent show, (l. to r.) Clara L. Sizer, Alice Wilson, Annette Roye, and Martha E Lewis. COURTESY MARGUERITE DAVIS JACKSON.

BACCALAUREATE AND COMMENCEMENT

Graduation was held in the chapel. We marched in as Mrs. Carter played the piano. Ms. Mayme Coleman (Jeanes' supervisor) was there. Graduation was somewhat sad because all of the boys who were over 18 were not there because they had been drafted I was the valedictorian of my class and gave a speech. My family did not have a car, so my father hitchhiked to school to attend graduation. I received a scholarship to Virginia Union University from the Union High Alumni Association. Rev. Thomas presented the scholarship to me. I could see my father's face. He was so proud.

Ivone Parker McReynolds
Class of 1944

Dr. Daniels, president of Virginia State College, was the speaker at our baccalaureate. There were 63 students in our class. I was the valedictorian.

Daisy Jackson Thomas
Class of 1950

Graduation was an exciting time. We were the first class to graduate from the new building. We were very proud.

Charles Gray
Class of 1952

We had a baccalaureate and commencement service. For the baccalaureate service, the top five students had to make a speech. I was fourth in the class. The teachers gave us the subjects, and we had to write a speech. They had to approve our speech and rehearsed us.

Sherrillyn LaVerne Smith Silver
Class of 1965

I was the first high school graduate from my family. All my family came to the ceremony; people from out of town (Maryland and D.C.). My mother's house was full with people, and my grandmother's house was full, too.

We had to wear a white dress for the baccalaureate service. My Uncle Eddie (Eddie Nelson) took me to Miller and Rhodes in Richmond and bought my dress. It was a two-piece dress. I also got shoes. I was really proud of being able to walk across the stage [at graduation].

Eleanor Thomas Hawkins.
Class of 1965

We practiced for graduation for about a month. We had to line up by height. We learned to put on our caps and how to walk together. The tassels swayed as we walked in unison. We practiced and practiced and practiced.

Geneva Johnson Thompson
Class of 1963
Business Teacher

FIELD TRIPS

We took educational field trips to Washington, D.C., and Richmond, Virginia. They were always one-day trips on the school buses. Parents did not have much money. Most parents had more than one child in school. We were well versed on government. We went to the White House, saw Congress and the Senate in action. We visited the Library of Congress, Smithsonian Museum, Washington Monument, Lincoln and Jefferson Memorials, and every educational place in our nation's capital.

Daisy Jackson Thomas
Class of 1950

Going on field trips was nice. They got us out of class. We went to museums in D.C. and the state fair in Richmond. Many students did not have transportation, so they [field trips] gave us an opportunity to see things we would normally not see.

Beulah Collins
Class of 1959

Eleanor Thomas with her parents, Thelma Thomas and Lee Roy Thomas, at her 1965 graduation.

We went to the Monument and the Capitol in Washington and Hershey Park. I enjoyed field trips because they were an opportunity to get out to see what existed outside Caroline County.

Aterita Baker Brown
Attended Union High from 1958 to 1961

We enjoyed school trips because they gave us the opportunity to get out of Caroline County. Most families did not take vacations, so school trips were the only time we got to leave the county. We went to the zoo in Washington, D.C., and the state fair in Richmond, Virginia. Mr. Beverly drove us on the school bus.

Eleanor Thomas Hawkins
Class of 1965

HOMECOMING

I was Miss Homecoming 1963–1964. This was the first year they had Miss Homecoming. I was elected by popular vote of the entire student body. I rode a car on the field during the homecoming game.

Sherrillyn LaVerne Smith Silver
Class of 1965

JUNIOR-SENIOR PROM

The junior-senior prom was held in the USO building. I did not go to the junior prom. The senior prom was great. I was escorted by a college student.

Daisy Jackson Thomas
Class of 1950

Prom was held in the USO building. In the 9th grade, my best friend Marlene Jackson and I were Candy Girls. We had a box with a ribbon that went around our necks and contained candy and gum. We walked around and let the prom guests select candy or gum at random.

Dorothy Samuels Jackson
Class of 1950

I did not go to the junior prom. I was head over heels in love with someone in the service. In my young mind, I was being faithful to him by not going to the prom. I went to the prom with Thomas Claiborne my senior year. He was the boyfriend of my friend Jackie Keys. He was in the service, and he surprised her by coming home to take her to the prom. She had already asked someone else [to go to the prom with her]. I was going to go [to the prom] alone because my boyfriend was still in the service. I went to the prom with Thomas so he could be at the prom with Jackie.

Eleanor Thomas Hawkins
Class of 1965

Sherrilynn LaVerne Smith, Miss Homecoming 1963–1964. SOURCE: 1964 UNION HIGH YEARBOOK.

Homecoming 1968 attendants, Miss Union High and Miss Football Sweetheart. SOURCE: 1969 UNION HIGH YEARBOOK.

We worked very hard to transform the gym into a nice place for our prom. It was very competitive—each class would try to outdo the class from the previous year. We made flowers out of tissue paper. We would put up chicken wire and stuff it with the tissue-paper flowers. The shop class made an arch. It would either be in the entrance way or used as the place where pictures were taken. We would string wire across the gym and drape crepe paper over them. There were colored lights.

Geneva Johnson Thompson
Class of 1963
Business Teacher

The junior-senior prom was held in the gym. I attended the prom in the 9th and 10th grades. Mr. Luckie took pictures at the prom. In the 9th grade, I helped him. In the 10th grade, I was a Candy Girl. I walked around and passed out party favors (candy). In the 11th grade, I raised money, decorated the gym, and attended the prom.

(l. to r.) Carolyn Jones, William Byrd, Gladys Fitzhugh at after prom breakfast. Courtesy Patricia Sizer Adams.

After the prom in our senior year, several of us (by invitation only) had breakfast at the home of Patricia Sizer (Adams). The food was prepared by Mr. and Mrs. Sizer. We had a great time and were allowed to stay out later than our normal midnight curfew. We had to attend school the next day (Friday) to practice for baccalaureate on that Sunday and graduation the next week. If we did not attend the practice, we were told that we would not graduate. Of course, we were all there.

Gladys Fitzhugh-Pemberton
Class of 1964

Our proms were always based on a theme. The gym was decorated, and we always had live bands. The girls wore long, formal gowns. Guys wore tuxes. My mother and two other mothers of my classmates got together and gave a party-breakfast for us; it was held at my home in Chilesburg right after the senior prom.

Patricia Sizer Adams
Class of 1964

Below: William Byrd and Patricia Sizer at the after prom breakfast. Courtesy Patricia Sizer Adams.

Above: Hall of Fame Class Couple Katrina Beverly and Carl Fields. Source: 1968 Union High Yearbook.

The senior prom was a major event. Making plans for the theme, decorating the gym, having a date, getting a prom gown, being allowed to travel to the prom with your date, and just being at the prom were exciting moments beyond measure. I was so excited also because I traveled to Washington, D.C., on the Greyhound bus to meet my older sister, Claudia Beverly, so she could buy my prom gown. It was soooooo beautiful! I felt like a queen in my white gown trimmed with pink roses and greenery around the upper waistline.

My date was Carl Fields. In the yearbook, we were named the class couple in the Hall of Fame. Some students weren't allowed to go on dates, so my father ended up not only being a teacher and chaperon at the prom but had to pick up a few students for the prom and carry them back.

Katrina Beverly Gill
Class of 1968

Courtesy Marguerite Davis Jackson.

Source: 1964 Union High Yearbook.

MAY DAY-FIELD DAY

I was Miss Union High in 1942 (not sure of year). I got a pretty royal-blue sweater with a red "U" on it. When I went to college, I put it in the cleaners, and it disappeared. It broke my heart. I wanted to save it for my children.

Ivone Parker McReynolds
Class of 1944

I was Miss Union High 1945. Each homeroom selected a person to represent them. Each person had to collect donations, and the person who raised the most money became Miss Union High. The students in my homeroom helped raise money. Mr. Luckie took pictures, and we sold our pictures for 10 cents. My parents helped raise money by selling ice cream. My relatives also gave money. I raised over $300 and was crowned Miss Union High in the spring during Field Day. As Miss Union High, I would travel with the baseball team to their games. There was no king and court at that time.

Susie Carter Quash
Class of 1947

May Day was a big festival. Parents and members of the community came to the school. Students would wrap the May Pole. The baseball game was in the evening. An ice truck would sell ice cream.

Clara Latney Hudson
Class of 1949

May Day was always a gala occasion, with the wrapping of the May Pole and girls in their paper dressed to match the colors of the May Pole. We did not have a Miss Union High, parade, or band. Field Day was always a great day because that was the only day we [girls] could wear pants. Other schools would come to compete in the games. There were sack races and competitions.

Daisy Jackson Thomas
Class of 1950

Ruby Monroe, 1954 Field Day. Her dress is made from crepe paper.
COURTESY BEULAH COLLINS

May Day was very enjoyable for me. I liked to watch the winding of the May Pole and the colorful floats. I would always try to have money for extra treats.

Dorothy Carter Black
Class of 1952

May Day was held in the spring on a Saturday. It was a big social event for the entire community. It was held in combination with the elementary school students. Students would wrap the May Pole, and a baseball game was held in the evening. It was a fundraiser for the school, refreshments were sold, and people had to pay to get in.

Calvin Taylor Sr.
Class of 1969

What is now referred to as May Day, we knew as Field Day. The traditional May Pole wrapping was done by the elementary school children. We did not have a May Queen or parade. The big event of the day was a game played by our baseball team against some team from another area, which, it was rumored, Mr. Ruffin selected because he knew we would win! And we always did.

Emma Samuel Vaughan
Class of 1950

Students and teachers work on May Day float decorations. COURTESY MARGUERITE DAVIS JACKSON.

Every year on the first Saturday in May, Union High would have a May Day celebration. There was a parade around the school with floats that were built by different organizations or clubs. Miss Union High was crowned. The day ended with a ball game between Union High School and another team.

Evelyn Wright Thompson
Class of 1958

May Day was a big affair. People who had gone away to college or moved away would come back. Family would come from all around. It was a day to reminisce and socialize. It started at 8 a.m. and ended in the evening with a baseball game.

Beulah Collins
Class of 1959

May Day was a big and exciting event. It was an event for the whole community—lots of people came. They closed Highway Number 2 for the parade. The band led the parade. I was a majorette and marched with the band. We marched from Bowling Green back to Union High. Everyone came out to see the parade—people would line up on both sides of the street. It was a nice time for socializing and eating.

Sherrillyn LaVerne Smith Silver
Class of 1965

May Day was looked forward to with great anticipation. We loved May Day. It was like a fair for the Black community, like a homecoming. People who had left the community to go to school or moved away would come back. Everyone wanted to look their best. They would get their hair done and put on a nice outfit. They guys would buy new Banlon shirts with matching socks (example, if they had a red shirt, they would wear red socks). There was a parade with the band, majorettes, and floats from the different organizations. There was the wrapping of the May Pole (I never was selected to wrap the May Pole), sack races, softball and baseball games.

Geneva Johnson Thompson
Class of 1963
Business Teacher

Regena Green, Miss Union High 1964. SOURCE: 1964 UNION HIGH YEARBOOK.

I was Miss Union High 1964. Representatives were picked from each grade. Students voted who should represent their grade. I was select to represent the 8th grade. The representatives were picked in October and had to do fundraising until April. The person who raised the most money won. My family helped me raise money. We had weenie roasts (sold hot dogs) and bake sales, sold dinners, and had a social at the dance hall. I also sold candy at school.

It was an honor to be Miss Union High. I was crowned at the May Day festival. I would travel with the sports teams to tournaments. At the VIAA tournament, they would announce all the queens [from the different schools] at half-time. We also had lunch with the coaches and tournament sponsors.

Regena Green Harris
Class of 1967

UHS CELEBRATES A FESTIVE MAY DAY

In spite of the grayish skies and intermittent rain, our May Day proceeded as planned. The frolicsome day began with a parade, which colored the day despite the dull clouds. The Mighty Marching Pointers led the way followed by and array of floats decorated in appropriate accents of flavor and color.

The most important of all was the royal float enhanced by the beauty of our Queen—Miss Tylle M. Goodall. This princess was robed in the symbol of purity with garlands of crimson roses in her hands. After the court returned to the campus, the Marching Pointers calmed the atmosphere with our "National Anthem." On the "Sound of Music," our class attendants, Miss Henrietta Anderson and Miss Louise B. Johnson. The cherubic flower girls Rinalda King and Vanessa Ferguson rolled out the beautifully vivid carpet of jewels carried by little M. Carson Jackson. After the coronation by Mr. Ruffin, the sparkling crown adorned the princess with indescribable grandeur.

After a brief rain intermission, the Queen was given a variety of entertainment. To begin the program were twelve charming ladies in gowns who wrapped our traditional May Pole. Adding a touch of variety were "The Swingers," followed by the stunts and tumbling which many found exciting. The "Square Dance" brought forth a Southern atmosphere, however, the "Go-Go" Dancers returned us to a variety of modern steps. The Marching Pointers climaxed the entertainment with a different exhibition of routines. The drummers came on with three swinging routines followed by the majorettes and the high-stepping Pointers. The audience sang as the band played our "Alma Mater." During the recessional of the queen and her attendants, the band played the "Sound of Music." In band formation the Mighty Marching Pointers left the field after fascinating the entire audience.

Diane Nelson

SOURCE: THE POINTER REVIEW, JUNE 1967

Varsity Float. Marguerite Jackson (third from left, with pearl necklace). Floats were decorated by taping crepe paper and streamers to chicken wire and tying the chicken wire to a car or truck. SOURCE: 1956 UNION HIGH YEARBOOK.

Clubs and Organizations

Clubs and organizations augmented the academic skills that were taught in the classroom and provided students with an opportunity to develop social and leisure skills. Teachers served as advisors for each club or organization.

Because of segregation, Negro and White schools did not compete against each other in sports or scholastic events. White high schools were members of the Virginia High School League, administered by the University of Virginia. This organization served as the central coordinating agency for school activities at White high schools in Virginia. There was no such organization for Negro high schools.

The principals of Negro high schools organized the Virginia Interscholastic Athletic League (VIAL), which allowed students from Negro schools to compete in statewide athletic programs. In 1954, the National Association of Secondary School Principals (an organization of principals for Negro high schools) urged Virginia State College to request the general assembly to appropriate funds for an organization to govern all nonacademic activities of Negro high schools in Virginia. The request was granted, and the Virginia Interscholastic Association (VIA) was formed.

In conjunction with the Division of Field Services at Virginia State College, the principals of the Negro secondary schools in Virginia administered the VIA. All Negro high schools in Virginia were eligible for membership. Annual membership that students paid provided money for oper-

ating activities. Schools were grouped into groups according to school enrollment, and the groups were further divided into regional districts.[75]

From April 1954 to August 1969, the VIA organized athletic programs and provided statewide competitions for baseball, basketball, track and field, golf, football, and tennis. They also had a film library for football, basketball, and baseball.

Band in the early 1960s. Courtesy Patricia Sizer Adams.

In addition to athletic competitions, they sponsored drama festivals and science and math competitions. The VIA also provided guidelines for establishing organizations and held state conferences for athletic associations, student council (via Student Participation Association), National Honor Society, and forensic activities.

From 1934 through 1955, the Music Conference of the Virginia Teachers Association (MCTVA) held state music festivals that allowed students from Negro high schools in Virginia to compete in orchestra, band, and choral events. In 1956, the MCTVA replaced the music festivals with the All State Music Program, which it co-sponsored with the Virginia Interscholastic Association (VIA) to improve the music program and encourage wider local participation.

As Virginia schools began to integrate in the 1960s, VIA membership declined. In August 1969, the Virginia Interscholastic Association ceased to exist after it merged with the previously White Virginia High School League.

BAND

The 1956–1957 school year was the first year for band. Teachers met with the parents to see who would be interested in being in the band. Mr. Jennings was the band teacher. The parents had to buy the instruments. I was in the band for two years—I played the clarinet. We were both a marching band and a concert band. The concert band performed in the auditorium; the marching band marched in the May Day parade. There were also majorettes. Our uniform was black bottoms (pants for boys, skirts for girls) and white tops.

Evelyn Wright Thompson
Class of 1958

My music teacher at Virginia State College was Dr. Gatlin. He would keep in contact with all his former students. He would call me to see if I

CLUB AND ORGANIZATION SUMMARY

Athletic Association
Barbering
Band
Cheerleaders
Chorus and Choir
Commerce Club
Commercial Club
Cosmetology
DECA
Dramatic Club
French Club
Future Business Leaders of America (FBLA)
New Farmers of America (NFA) and Future Farmers of America (FFA)
New Homemakers of America (NHA) and Future Homemakers of America (FHA)
Library Club and Future Librarians of America (FLA)
Hall Patrol
Home Economics Club
Industrial Arts Club
Literary Club
Masonry Club
Majorettes
Modern Dance Group (The Rhythm Stars)
National Honor Society
Patrol
Pep Squad
Physical Education Club
Science Club
Student Council and Student Government
Ushers
Yearbook Staff

had a student who could play a particular instrument when he had a need for the instrument in his band. I would select some students to go and play with the Virginia State band.

Blonnie Tipton
Band Director

1956–1957 band, William Jennings, director. Evelyn Wright Thompson is the second person from the left in the second row. SOURCE: *1957 UNION HIGH YEARBOOK.*

In May 1963, the Union High School band, under the direction of Blonnie Tipton, recorded a record consisting of "Stranger on the Shore" (Mellin and Bilk), "Tangotoon" (Kinyon), "The Fairest of the Fair" (Sousa), "Lazy Day" (Piato).

I enjoyed being in the band. We traveled and competed against other bands. It was our opportunity to see the world outside of Caroline County.
Vernelle Twiggs
Class of 1967

I played the clarinet in the band at Union High. I went on tour with the Virginia State College Band my senior year in high school. Dr. Gatlin [director of Virginia State College Music Department] contacted Mrs. Tipton, who was a former student of his, because he needed a tenor saxophone player. I did not know how to play the tenor sax, but it was an easy transition from clarinet to the saxophone. With Mrs. Tipton's help, I learned the music and went on tour. The tour was in the spring and lasted about a week. We toured all of the northeastern states from Virginia to Massachusetts. We stayed in the homes of Virginia State alumni in each state. It

was quite an experience. I decided to major in music when I attended college because I was impressed by the teaching ability of Mrs. Tipton and the many enriching experiences I had while in the band at Union High.
Patricia Sizer Adams
Class of 1964

Performing in the band gave me confidence and helped develop my self-esteem. The band would travel to the state competitions to contend with schools from all over Virginia. We often would take first place. It felt good to be a little country school and beat bands from the city.
Beryl Jackson
Attended Union High from 1963 to 1965
Graduated from Caroline High in 1968

Being a member of the band taught me discipline, organizational and planning skills, and gave me confidence.
William Brawner
Class of 1966

1962–1963 marching band and majorettes, Blonnie Tipton, band director. COURTESY BLONNIE TIPTON.

1965–1966 concert band as they appeared in concert for the Virginia Teachers Association. Source: Union High 1966 Yearbook.

Mr. Bennett was a young guy from college, and the students liked him because he was young and hip. The band played modern music. The band performed in the Thalhimers Parade in Richmond and the Tobacco Festival Parade.

Arthur Sizer Jr. Attended Union High 1967–1969 Graduated from Ladysmith High 1972

CHEERLEADERS AND PEP SQUAD

Cheerleaders provided school spirit during athletic events. The pep squad assisted the cheerleaders by cheering from the stands, not the floor or field.

Cheerleaders and Pep Squad Source: 1967 Union High Yearbook

Source: 1958 Union High Yearbook.

CHORAL CLUB, CHORUS, AND CHOIR

My participation in the chorus was exceedingly enriching. Under the direction of Mrs. Carter, we compiled quite a varied repertory of music. Sometimes we performed for community functions, but our main performances were at the commencement programs. I learned to appreciate many kinds of music through my participation in the chorus.

I once had a rather disconcerting experience as a participant of the chorus. During our performance at commencement, I was to render the solo part of one of the selections. When the time came for me to sing my part, my mind went blank. After a couple of false starts, Mrs. Carter, our director, hummed the first chord, thus releasing my mental block. I felt sure that the other students would tease me to the point of tears because of my blunder, but actually, no one mentioned it, not even Mrs. Carter. We sang the selection a cappella, so apparently no one noticed it. Following the performance, a group of students came up to me shouting, "Gosh, Loureve, I didn't know you could sing like that!" Their words were like music to my ears, and my letdown feeling instantly dissipated.[76]

Florence Coleman Bryant
Class of 1940

I sang in the choir. We had several choir directors: Miss Betty Banks when I was in the 8th grade; another lady for a short time (I can't remember her name), and Mr. I. D. Ruffin in the 9th, 10th, and 11th grades. They all did a fine job of picking the most beautiful music. We sang "You'll Never Walk Alone" by Fred Waring, "Deep River," "The Lord is My Light and My Salvation," and so on. It was such a joy to be in the choir; we mainly sang for school functions (assemblies, graduation, etc.)
Dorothy Samuels Jackson
Class of 1950

The Alma Mater was written by Mr. Shelby Guss and Ms. Jewel Taylor. Mr. Guss wrote the words, and Miss Taylor wrote the music. I sang the solo part during 1957–1958. The choir had a Christmas concert and participated in the choir festival in the spring. We always won first place.
Barbara Jones Rock
Class of 1961

Union High chorus 1930s or 1940s. COURTESY WESLEY T. CARTER.

SOURCE: *1950 UNION HIGH YEARBOOK.*

I enjoyed being in the choir. Each year we went to the choir festival in Richmond. Mrs. Wilson was the choir director. She was very passionate. We would rehearse for a long time and focus on proper breathing, pronunciation, holding our mouths correctly to get the correct sound. The choir festival was one day. We would compete with different schools in Virginia. We sang sacred and secular songs. It was very exciting.

Geneva Johnson Thompson
Class of 1963
Business Teacher

COMMERCIAL CLUB
COMMERCE CLUB
FUTURE BUSINESS LEADERS OF AMERICA

Organized in 1950, the Commercial Club consisted of students from the commercial science class. In the 1960s, Union High formed a chapter of the Future Business Leaders of America (FBLA) that included all students in the business and commercial classes.

I got my foundation from clubs and organizations. They taught me leadership skills. I joined the Future Business Leaders of America in the 8th grade and Phi Beta Lambda in college. I am a life member. I was a member of the boards of directors from 1993 to 1997 and FBLA chair in 1995.

Gladys Fitzhugh-Pemberton
Class of 1964

I was a member of the FBL. Miss Easter was an inspiration—we developed a kinship with her. We liked the way she carried herself. I said when I grew up I wanted to be just like her. I knew I wanted to go to college and major in business education. That is why I came back and taught [after college], to give back to my community. I taught for 27 years.

Geneva Johnson Thompson
Class of 1963
Business Teacher

Future Business Leaders of America. Gladys Fitzhugh (with glasses) is front row center. SOURCE: 1964 UNION HIGH YEARBOOK.

THE DRAMATICS CLUB
By Jessica Lewis

Members of the Dramatics Club presented their first production of the year with "The First Thanksgiving," an Episode from a pageant of Pilgrims by Esther Will Bates. The play was based on the First Thanksgiving. Mrs. Satterwhite gave an opinion of the way she interpreted the play. She said, "The play showed that the people of those days, loved, became angry, danced, and suffered many hardships as the people of today."

Wednesday, December 20, 1961, the Dramatics Club will present a pantomime of the nativity scene. The pantomime deals with Christmas, the time celebrated because of the birth of Christ. The pantomime will be presented with the participation of the Union High School's Choir Singing "O Holy Night," the Band and the Physical Education Department's Dance Groups, a Speech Chorus of Eleventh Graders, and the Dramatics group pantomiming "O Holy Night" consisting of Virgin Mary, Joseph and Shepherds.

We hope you will enjoy and be inspired by it.

President, James Johnson, Director, Mr. E. A. Austin

SOURCE: UNION HERALD, DECEMBER 22, 1961

SOURCE: 1955
UNION HIGH
YEARBOOK

LIBRARY CLUB
FUTURE LIBRARIANS
OF AMERICA

In the early years, the organization was called the Library Club. Later, Union High developed a chapter of the Future Librarians of America (FLA). The organization taught students library procedures and techniques, popularized reading among all students, and provided an understanding of the library profession.

SOURCE: 1955 UNION HIGH YEARBOOK.

Literary Club members prepare to record "The Road Not Taken" by Robert Frost. SOURCE: 1957 UNION HIGH YEARBOOK.

LITERARY CLUB

The Literary Club stimulated an interest in reading.

MAJORETTES

I was a majorette in the 8th grade and later became head majorette. The majorettes went everywhere the band went. In the early 1960s, Virginia Union did not have a band. The Union High band and majorettes performed at their half-time.

Regena Green Harris
Class of 1967

NATIONAL HONOR SOCIETY

Members for the National Honor Society were selected based on Scholarship, Service, Leadership, and Character. They pledged to be honest and search for the truth, as well as strive for outstanding academic achievement.

National Honor Society. SOURCE: 1969 UNION HIGH YEARBOOK.

Regena Green (center) performs with the Union High band during Virginia Union's Homecoming. SOURCE: 1966 UNION HIGH YEARBOOK.

New Farmers of America
Future Farmers of America

In the 1940s, Union High organized a chapter of the New Farmers of America that consisted of all students in the agriculture classes. It was the Negro counterpart to the Future Farmers of American, which did not grant membership to Negro students. The group was a member of the larger state and national organization.

The New Farmers of America Creed was:

NFA exhibit won 1st place at the September 1960 Virginia State Fair in Richmond, Virginia. SOURCE: 1961 UNION HIGH YEARBOOK.

I believe in the dignity of farm work and that I shall prosper in proportion as I learn to put knowledge and skill into the occupations of farming.

I believe that the farm boy who learns to produce better crops and better livestock; who learns to improve and beautify his home surroundings will find joy and success in meeting the challenging situations as they arise in his daily living.

I believe that rural organizations should develop their leaders from within; that the boys in the rural communities should look forward to positions of leadership in the civic, social and public life surrounding them.

I believe that the life of service is the life that counts; that happiness endures to mankind when it comes from having helped lift the burdens of others.

I believe in the practice of cooperation in agriculture; that it will aid in bringing to the man lowest down a wealth of giving as well as receiving.

I believe that each farm boy bears the responsibility for finding and developing his talents to the end that the life of his people may thereby be enriched so that happiness and contentment will come to all.[77]

New Farmers of America. SOURCE: 1956 UNION HIGH YEARBOOK.

New Homemakers of America representatives model dresses in sewing competition at the state convention.
COURTESY ERCELLE DEYO BYRD.

In the 1960s as schools throughout the United States began to integrate, the New Farmers of America merged with the Future Farmers of America.

NEW HOMEMAKERS OF AMERICA
FUTURE HOMEMAKERS OF AMERICA

All students in the home economics classes made up the Union High chapter of the New Homemakers of America (NHA) organized in the 1940s. It was the Negro counterpart to the Future Homemakers of America, which did not grant membership to Negro students. The group was a member of the larger state and national organization.

The purpose of the New Homemakers of America was to:

Promote individual growth by developing physical, social and moral qualities

Promote better home living

Promote wholesome recreational activities

To act as a unit for giving service to the school, community, state and nation[78]

The New Homemakers of American Creed was:

We, the New Homemakers of America believe that—

If there is kindness and truth in the heart,

There will be beauty in the spirit.

If there is beauty in the spirit,

There will be harmony and love in the home.

If there is harmony and love in the home,

There will be justice in the Nation

If there is justice in the Nation,

There will be peace in the world.[79]

As schools throughout the United States began to integrate, in 1965 the New Homemakers of America merged with the Future Homemakers of America.

Mrs. Banks selected Elisha Rock, Etoye Morton, Ercelle Deyo, Alleen Morton, and me to represent Union High at the NHA state convention at Virginia State. Students from schools all over the state competed in a sewing competition. Before going to the convention, we each made a princess-line dress with a square neckline. The dress had an eyelet outline that was accented with contrasting ribbon. We worked very hard on the dresses. Mrs. Ragland was a senior at Virginia State then. She helped us put the final touches on our dresses. We won first place. Mrs. Banks was shocked and surprised—she was so happy.

Ivone Parker McReynolds
Class of 1946

1964 NHA Conference in Houston, Texas. Sherrillynn LaVerne Smith is second row third from the left. COURTESY SHERRILLYNN LAVERNE SMITH SILVER.

in Virginia too. We rode the train for 3 days and 3 nights. We did not have a sleeper car, so we sat up the entire time and took cat naps when we could. At the convention, I went to meetings and met other students from schools from other states. It was extremely hot. We stayed in the school dormitory, and there was no air conditioner.

I learned public speaking from being NHA president. The installation of the officers was a big event. It was held in the auditorium. I had to tell each new officer her duties and responsibilities. I memorized what I had to say instead of reading it. Mrs. Ragland thought that was a good idea.

Sherrillyn LaVerne Smith Silver
Class of 1965

I was president of the Union High NHA and vice president of the state NHA. In 1965, the NHA and FHA merged. I became member at large of FHA. I attended a national conference at Langston University in Langston, Oklahoma. The state advisor, Ms. Grace Harris, and Mrs. Banks went with me. We rode the train from Richmond to Oklahoma. I attended leadership training and worked on projects. I got along with everyone at the FHA national convention.

Evelyn Ragland
Class of 1967

I was NHA president my senior year (1964–1965). I was voted into office in the spring of 1964. In June of 1964, I attended the national conference in Houston, Texas, at Texas Southern University and represented Union High. My parents drove me to the train station in Richmond, and I caught the train to Texas. There were other students from schools

COTTON BALL

Friday, April 14, 1961, the Union Chapter of New Homemakers of America ended its celebration of the National NHA Week by sponsoring a Cotton Ball. The theme for our cotton ball was "The Cotton Merry-Go-Round."

A huge cotton ball extended from the center of the ceiling of the cafeteria from which hung streamers of cotton materials. Small NHA emblems were attached to the end of the streamers, which helped to carry out our theme.

Refreshments consisted of fruit punch, assorted cookies, and mints.

Music was furnished by the Souvenirs, which was composed of several students of our school. The music rendered was enjoyed by all.

The girls looked beautiful in their cotton dresses, and the boys were charming in their dark suits.

Sister NHA'ers wish to express their appreciation to the cotton ball committee who worked so diligently to make their affair a success.

SOURCE: UNION HERALD, APRIL 28, 1961

NEWSPAPER CLUB

The Union High news paper had several names over the years: The Pointer (1950), The Union Script (1959), The Union Herald (1961).

Union High newspaper The Pointer, December 1950.
COURTESY CASSANDRA DAVIS BROWN.

UNION HIGH SCHOOL JOINS HONORARY SOCIETY
By Wendell Byrd

Union High recently was accepted as a member of the Quill and Scroll International Honorary Society for High School Journalists. The Quill and Scroll Society was founded at the State University of Iowa in 1926. Union High was accepted as a result of the yearbook submitted this year. Membership in this society gives Union authority to establish and perpetuate a chapter of Quill and Scroll. I believe that acceptance into this society will benefit both the newspaper staff and the patrons reading our paper by stimulating us to produce the best possible publication at all times.

A chapel program is in the making for the presentation of the charter to the entire school.

SOURCE: UNION HERALD, NOVEMBER 13, 1961

Newspaper Club. SOURCE 1959 UNION HIGH YEARBOOK.

SCIENCE CLUB

Science Club. SOURCE: 1958 UNION HIGH YEARBOOK.

STUDENT COUNCIL
STUDENT GOVERNMENT

The Student Council and Student Government consisted of two representatives from each homeroom and elected officers. Officer positions were president, vice president, secretary, assistant secretary, treasurer, parliamentarian, captain of patrols, and sergeant at arms. Students campaigned for officer positions and were elected by the majority vote. The organizations were intended to stimulate school spirit.

Student Council. 1962 Union High Yearbook.

YEARBOOK

In the early years, Union High students created a yearbook by pasting their personal photographs on paper, handwriting the captions, and typing the other pages. With the exception of 1951 (when there was no senior class), Union High published a Yearbook every from 1949 to 1969. The first hardcover year book was published in 1953.

I was the senior class secretary and worked on the yearbook with the other senior class officers. Only the principal, teachers, and senior class officers knew what we were doing. We were told the information was not to be shared. As a matter of fact, when I was working on the yearbook, they locked me in the principal's office so no one could see what I was working on. I did a lot of the typing on the yearbook. I also did some of the drawing and the captions under the pictures. The yearbook was passed out to the students close to graduation.

Cassandra Marie Davis Brown
Class of 1950

Yearbook staff. Source: *1953 Union High Yearbook.*

Athletics

The athletic programs, especially baseball, brought Union High notoriety in Caroline County and Virginia, serving as a form of entertainment for the school and the community.

Early athletics at the school included baseball, volleyball, basketball, tennis, and croquet teams, and the campus contained a diamond or court for these activities.[80] By the late 1930s, the athletic program was suffering. When George Ruffin was hired in 1939 as a social studies teacher, he was also given the responsibility of reviving the program and coaching the baseball team. At that time, the only equipment for the team was a broken bat and one mitt. There were no team uniforms. Ruffin raised $56 for equipment and purchased team shirts for $1 each. The team's first season was not very successful—they won only three games.[81]

Walter E. Lowe became coach of the baseball team in 1939, when Ruffin was promoted to principal. The team was not very well organized at that time. The players had to buy their own uniforms or use money donated by local business, so the team uniforms were often mismatched. There was no formal method for communicating the team's schedule. Instead, the time and location of games was spread through the community by word of mouth.

Despite these shortcomings, the baseball team evolved into a championship team under Lowe's leadership. During his 24 years of coaching, the team won 224 games and lost 20.[82] The team won the Tidewater Interscholastic Athletic Association (TIAA) championship every year from 1941 through 1950. In 1950 and 1951, the team had a 72-game winning streak. They won the Virginia Interscholastic Athletic League State Championship during the 1950, 1951, 1962, and 1964 seasons.[83]

1943 Girls' softball and boys' baseball teams. Courtesy Marguerite Davis Jackson.

In the later years, the Union High athletic program consisted of baseball, basketball (girls and boys), and softball. In 1964, football was added. Union High did not have a football field, so they played all their home games on the field at Caroline High School.

When I first came to Union High [in 1939], Rev. Hovey R. Young was the principal, and Mr. George B. Ruffin was the baseball coach. I was the assistant baseball coach. I also coached basketball. At that time, the school did not have a gym, so the basketball team played their games outside. By the end of the year, Rev. became ill, and Mr. Ruffin became the principal. Mr. Ruffin did not have time to be the principal and the coach. I became the baseball coach.

In the beginning, we had to raise money for everything. The school board did not give the team any money. I would solicit donations from businesses in Caroline County and a few in Fredericksburg and Richmond. At some point in the late 1950s or early 1960s, the Athletic Association became more active. They took over the fundraising, buying uniforms and equipment.

During my time as the baseball coach, we won 224 games and lost 20. We had a 72-game winning streak and won numerous TIAA and VIAA championships. When Union High won the VIAA State Championship in the 1950s, we were the first school (Black or White) in Caroline County to win a state championship. Earl Richards, William Johnson, John Beverly, and [could not remember his first name] Samuels were some of the members of that championship team.

One year, I took some of the players to Washington, D.C., to see Howard University play North Carolina AT &T at the old Griffith Stadium because two former players were playing. James Purce was playing for Howard University, and Earl Richards was playing for North Carolina AT &T. A parent volunteered to take some of the students. We did not have to pay any admission because we were a team. The students enjoyed the trip.

BASKETBALL (BOYS)

(l. to r.) Front: Charles Woodfork, William "Tip Top" Johnson, John "Gravy" Graves, Edward Peterson, Earl Richards, and Thomas Ware; back: Percy Samuels, unknown, Coach Walter Lowe, Wilson "Heavy" Wilson, Thomas Wright. SOURCE: 1950 UNION HIGH YEARBOOK.

THE MIGHTY POINTERS BASKETBALL TEAM
J. L. Hicks, Coach

SOURCE: 1968 UNION HIGH YEARBOOK.

I also coached basketball from the 1940s until some time in the 1950s. The athletic teams, especially the baseball team, brought attention to Union High. The team kept the school in the news. People were very interested in the team. I told my players it was their responsibility to support the school and keep it in a positive light. I had nice students, they did not cause trouble.

I did not get paid for coaching until my last year. I used my own money to buy items for the players and would take players home who did not have rides. I did not have an assistant coach, but Earl Richards would help out. I retired from coaching at the end of the 1965 season when I became assistant principal. Mr. Earl Richards became the baseball coach. I enjoyed coaching. I did my best, loved what I did, and the players respected me.

Mr. Ruffin appointed me director of athletics in 1940 after I had taken over coaching baseball and basketball when he became principal. My first responsibility was to contact other rural schools and organize the Tidewater Interscholastic Athletic Association for baseball and basketball. We developed the rules for the conference regarding school attendance, grades, and age requirements. Originally, the conference was only for boy's baseball and basketball. Girl's softball and basketball were added later. I stopped being the director of athletics in the early 1960s.

Dr. Walter E. Lowe
Industrial Arts Teacher
Assistant Principal
Coach

BASKETBALL (GIRLS)

TIAA Girl's Basketball Champions, season record: 23-0. SOURCE: 1955 UNION HIGH YEARBOOK.

SOURCE: 1963 UNION HIGH YEARBOOK

BASEBALL

The boys' baseball team, coached by Mr. Lowe, never lost a game while I was in high school. I am aware that some of the players were offered the opportunity to play pro ball but passed up the offer to continue their education. The entire team graduated with the Class of 1950, and when they marched into the auditorium for graduation, Coach Lowe had tears in his eyes!

Emma Samuel Vaughan
Class of 1950

I played on the baseball team. We got to the semifinals in 1962. Mr. Walter Lowe was the coach. He did not believe in us staying out late. We had to be in bed by 8 p.m. He also made sure we did our class work.

Elmer Johnson
Class of 1962

1947–1948 baseball team, (l. to r.) front: John Smith, James "Jimmy" Purce, Franke Phillips, [George?] Monroe, Lumell Berry; back: Eugene "Jack" Claiborne, William Young, Frank Johnson, Walter Lowe (coach), Don Redd, "Skeeter" Saunders, "Dickey" Sales. COURTESY LOUISE BOONE YOUNG.

State championships, (l. to r.) front: W. Williams, A. Beynum, R. Jefferson, W. Reynolds, R. Redd, J. Garner, C. Byrant, J. Young; back: Walter Lowe (coach), J. T. Williams (student manager and assistant coach), C. Washington, George Coleman, J. Jeter, R. Johnson, Joe Brown, J. Shelby Guss (publicity manager) , and George Ruffin (principal). SOURCE: 1956 UNION HIGH YEARBOOK.

FOOTBALL

SOURCE: (ABOVE) *1964 UNION HIGH YEARBOOK*. (AT RIGHT) *1958 UNION HIGH SCHOOL YEARBOOK*

SOFTBALL

I was the pitcher on the softball team for four years. The team never lost a game.
Gladys Rich Ferguson
Class of 1941

(l. to r.) Front: Beverly Johnson, Dorothy Howard, Emma Samuel, Thelma Williams, Mariah Moore, Back Row Dorothy Samuels, Mary Fortune, Mr. Lloyd Boxley (coach), Dorothy Carter, Dorothy Dudley. Source: *1950 UNION HIGH SCHOOL YEARBOOK*.

One of my most vivid memories of playing on the girls' softball team involved a trip to King and Queen Country for a game. We went in two cars—I was in the front car driven by Mr. Lowe. Once when we looked back at the other car, driven by Coach Boxley, it had turned over. Fortunately, no one was hurt, but we missed the game.
Emma Samuel Vaughan
Class of 1950

Community

Union High was an important institution to the Negro community in Caroline County, Virginia. Social and civic organizations used the facility as a meeting place. The school also provided social activities such as dances and movies for the entire community.

In turn, members of the community worked hard to support Union High School. Many Union High faculty were leaders in the community—ministers, Sunday school teachers, business owners.

COUNTYWIDE LEAGUE AND PARENT TEACHERS ASSOCIATION

The Countywide League, which later evolved into the Parent Teacher Association (PTA), worked with the Sunday School Union to provide educational opportunities for the children. The PTA held fundraisers to buy school supplies and provide items needed by clubs and organizations such as band instruments, choir robes, and the Library Fund.

(Top) Original cannery. COURTESY PAULINE S. BOXLEY.
(Middle. l. to r.) A. McKee Banks, cannery manager and Union High agricultural teacher; Johnnie Washington (reaching up), cannery supervisor; Raymond Snead, superintendent of schools; Mary Washington, cannery worker. COURTESY PAULINE S. BOXLEY.
(Bottom) New Cannery. PHOTO BY MARION WOODFORK SIMMONS, OCTOBER 25, 2009

UNION HIGH ALUMNI ASSOCIATION

The Union High Alumni Association allowed alumni to remain in touch after graduation, to support the school, and to participate in social activities. There were chapters in various areas of Caroline County (Bowling Green, Central Point, Ruther Glen, Dawn, Woodford, Milford, Balty, St. John, File, St James, Sparta), as well as in Philadelphia, Pennsylvania, and Washington, D.C.

CAROLINE COMMUNITY CANNERY

During World War II, many communities in America suffered food shortages because the government rationed food. There were also labor and transportation shortages that made it difficult to harvest food and transport it to market. The government encouraged citizens to plant victory gardens to produce their own fruits and vegetables. Families were encouraged to save commercial canned goods for the troops and can their own vegetables.

In 1942, the state government started a program to send pressure cookers to rural communities to allow the citizens to preserve food from their victory gardens. The state department of education designated eight centers to receive a pressure cooker. The agricultural and home economics teachers supervised the project, but nonteaching staff managed the centers. The centers were given pressure cookers, but they had only wood stoves that could not be regulated. A. McKee Banks, an agricultural teacher, obtained money from the Sunday School Union to purchase oil burners that the agricultural teacher carried from center to center for one- or two-day canning sessions.

In 1944, the Caroline School Board authorized the use of school funds to supplement federal money for constructing and equipping canneries at Caroline and Union High Schools under the Rural War Production Training Act.[84] Members of the Negro community raised additional capital to purchase the supplies. Union High students and staff volunteered to help with the remodeling and installation. Both Negro and White members of the community used the cannery. In the later years, Lloyd Boxley, another agricultural teacher, supervised the cannery, which he continued after his retirement. After his death in 2005, the cannery was renamed the Lloyd Boxley Cannery.

Club 18

In the 1950s, several Union High teachers and business owners established Club 18, a social club that organized activities for the community. Members of Club 18 were:

J. Shelby and Lavinia Guss–Teachers

Lloyd and Pauline Boxley–Teachers

Paul and Ethel Lowe–Teachers

McKee and Mary Banks–Teachers

Club 18 at a Dance.
Courtesy Pauline Boxley.

Walter and Fraulein Lowe–Teachers and Business Owners

Edward and Celestine Ragland–Teachers

Joseph and Lucille Johnson–Farm Agent

Joseph and Mary Adams–Business Owner and Funeral Director

Community Services

Members of the community used the services of the vocational education classes. Temporary medical clinics were setup at the school for community medical and dental services. Adult night classes allowed members of the community to take classes to obtain a GED and obtain better employment.

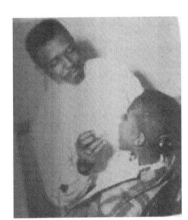

(Left) Dr. V. R. Roberts, school dentist.
Source: 1954 Union High Yearbook.

(Middle) Source: 1968 Union High Yearbook.

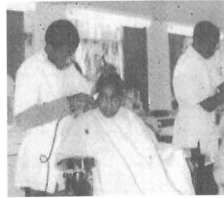

(Below) 1968 night typing class at Union High. Geneva Johnson is teacher.
Courtesy Beulah Collins.

Courtesy Marguerite Davis Jackson.

USO Highway Number 2

During Word War II, a large detachment of Negro troops arrived at the AP Hill Military Reservation for pre-combat training. Because of the segregationist policies of the times, these soldiers were not allowed to use the Court House Square USO facility. With members of the Negro community, the Union High administration and faculty stepped in to fill the void. They organized parties for the soldiers in their homes and held events for them in the school's auditorium.

In 1943, one acre of land was donated from the property of Union High School to build a USO facility for the Negro soldiers. Union High School served as the temporary location until the facility was completed.

George B. Ruffin and several Union High teachers were members of the USO Operating Committee. The USO director spoke at the Union High commencement and on many occasions was a guest speaker at the school's chapel service. The Union High junior-senior prom and several other school functions were held in the facility.

When the facility was closed in the late 1940s, the property was returned to the Caroline School Board for use by Union High. In the 1950s after the high school grades moved to the new building, the primary grades were taught in the old USO building.

The PTA was active. Some parents were very active in the school and community. I later realized that a lot of parents did not have transportation and a lived a long ways from Union High [that is why they were not active in the school].

Daisy Jackson Thomas
Class of 1950

The whole community was about education. They were very supportive and interested in the children. They would ask, "How are you doing in school?" "What did you get on your report card?" At the end of the school year they would ask, "Did you pass?" The baccalaureate service and graduation were attended by members of the community, even people who did not have a child graduating. I am so grateful for my parents and for all the parents and the community, for they gave to us the best of themselves. Their desire was to see their children have an opportunity to learn and to grow in ways that they never had an opportunity to do.

Dorothy Samuels Jackson
Class of 1950

During Thanksgiving and Christmas, the students would bring in food and make baskets. Each homeroom would make a basket. The students would bring in the names of people from the community who needed help and give them to the teacher. The teachers would deliver the baskets to the families.

Beulah Collins
Class of 1959

Union High was a pillar of the community, and the community was very supportive. Parents in the community would give rides to students who did not have transportation so they could attend school functions that were after school hours. People in the community would help the school raise money by donating all the items needed for fundraising. This reduced the expenses and allowed all the money raised from the sale of items to go to the school. The businesses in the community supported the school by purchasing ads and becoming patrons for the yearbook. I sold so many ads and got so many patrons I was able to get a free yearbook.

Catherine Ferguson
Class of 1969

Infrequently movies were shown in the auditorium. We had to pay to seem them. I enjoyed the movies at school. I did not like to go to the movies in Bowling Green because I would have to sit in the balcony. There were no restrictions on seats at school. Sometimes a guy would want to pay your way so that he could sit beside you.

Dorothy Carter Black
Class of 1952

SOURCE: UNION HIGH YEARBOOK.

Desegregation:
The Beginning of Change

On May 17, 1954, the U.S. Supreme Court ruled in *Brown vs. Board of Education of Topeka, Kansas* that separate educational facilities were inherently unequal, thus making separate schools for Negro and White students unconstitutional. Despite the ruling, the Caroline County school system, like many other Southern school systems, continued to operate as a segregated school system.

On February 26, 1965, the Caroline County School Board agreed to sign an Assurance of Compliance Pledge under Title IV of the Civil Rights Act of 1964.[85] The school board also implemented a Freedom of Choice plan in May of the same year that called for assigning pupils in all schools and all grades "without reference to race, color or national origin of any individual."[86]

At the beginning of the 1965–1966 school year, four students requested transfers from Union High to Caroline High.[87] No White students transferred from the White high schools, but some White teachers came to Union High.

As previously White national organizations began to accept Negro students, some of the Negro national organizations ceased to exist. Some teachers with long tenure at Union

President Lyndon B. Johnson signs the 1964 Civil Rights Act as Martin Luther King, Jr., others look on. SOURCE: CECIL STOUGHTON, WHITE HOUSE PRESS OFFICE/LBJ LIBRARY PHOTO LAB

High retired, and others left the school system to take advantage of new opportunities.

On August 28, 1968, the Caroline County NAACP filed a suit in the U.S. District Court in Richmond, Virginia, charging the Caroline County School system with failing to end racial discrimination in the county schools.[88] NAACP chapters from five other counties in Virginia filed similar suits and asked the federal court to order the school boards to eliminate racial segregation throughout their system, including personnel and transportation facilities.[89] In response to the lawsuit, Judge Robert R. Merhig Jr. ordered Caroline's Freedom of Choice program abandoned and an alternate method for integrating the schools developed.[90]

The teachers asked some of the honor students if they wanted to transfer to Caroline High. I was one of the students asked. I told my father I had been offered the opportunity to transfer to Caroline. He asked me if I wanted to go, and I said no. That was the end of the conversation. I am sure if I wanted to transfer to Caroline High, my Dad would have supported that decision too.

I chose to remain at Union High because I was receiving a good education there. Most important, the teachers believed in us and expected great accomplishments from us. I was not sure that the White teachers held that same opinion of us. It was my one life, and I did not have time for anyone (especially teachers), who might undermine my abilities. I had been with some of my classmates since the 1st grade and others since the 6th grade. It did not make sense for me to leave Union and go to another school just because the people there were White. There was no advantage to going to Caroline High. Caroline High did not have anything that was better than Union High. The county was not wealthy, so they could not afford to purchase a better set of books at one school and an inferior set for another school. We used the same textbooks approved by the school board. In fact, in those days, the parents purchased the books. Our parents purchased our books new from the publishers. Union High had a section of the library or the office where we paid for and picked up our new books. They were shipped in big boxes directly from the publishing companies to our school.

The Caroline High School building was much older than ours. Their teachers were no smarter than ours. I thought it would be a disadvantage to leave teachers and students I knew for those who would resent my desegregating their environment. Most important, because it was my last year in high school, I wanted to see where I placed among the honor students I had competed with at Union High. In fact, I was #4 out of 110 (My best friend, Goldie, now deceased, was #3).

Williabel Jones Davis
Class of 1966

I was not interested in transferring to Caroline High. I was ready to graduate. I had a lot of pride in going to Union. I felt love, comfort, and commitment at Union.

Carolyn Garnett Epps
Class of 1966

At the end of 11th grade, I learned that schools were integrating. Students were given the opportunity to transfer to Caroline High School, where the student body consisted of White students. At that point in my education, I firmly knew that I wanted to complete my high school education at Union High School. The next year I would be a senior and graduating. I knew that I wanted to be a 1968 graduate of Union High School!!!! I had a rich heritage, and I was not about to embark upon that [desegregating a White high school] my senior year of high school.

Katrina Beverly Gill
Class of 1968

I never thought about transferring to another school. I thought Union was a better school—it was newer and more modern. The teachers were part of the community, and they cared about us. All our family had gone to Union and had some of the same teachers. It never crossed my mind to go to another school. We had some White teachers. They fit in well. The students and teachers got along with them.

Catherine Ferguson
Class of 1969

Not that many students transferred [from Union] during Freedom of Choice. I never considered transferring to a White school. I thought Union High was better for me. I did not think transferring was necessary. When it was time to integrate, I did not have a problem with that either. But when I had a choice, I chose to stay at Union.

Arthur Sizer Jr.
Attended Union High 1967–1969
Graduated from Ladysmith High 1972

I learned about Freedom of Choice from attending the NAACP meetings. My family was very active in the NAACP. Martin Luther King and Thurgood Marshall would come to the meetings and talk to us about *Brown vs. Board of Education*. I decided to transfer to Caroline High School because I saw it as an opportunity to break down racial barriers. At that time, it was thought that White students were smarter than Black students. I wanted to prove a point that Blacks were just as smart as Whites and they could achieve as much as Whites if they were given the same opportunity. I also believed that if the opportunity was not taken, then desegregation might not happen. The Freedom of Choice Plan was set up because White people knew none of their children would attend an all-Black school and I think they thought we would be too afraid to attend theirs.

I had a variety of thoughts when I decided to transfer to Caroline High. I was afraid that I would not be able to compete with the Caroline High students. I was afraid for my physical safety and afraid of stepping into the unknown. I was sad because I was leaving my friends, the band, and people I had known all of my life. I had friends at Union High that I had known since the 1st grade. I was very popular and comfortable at Union. Union High was like a family I was going to leave to venture into the enemy's territory.

The reactions from members of the community and my friends were varied. Some people said I thought I was White, I thought I was better than them, and so on. After I transferred to Caroline High, I felt alone. I did not fit into Caroline High, but I was alienated from the Union High students in my community, in that I no longer hung with them on a daily basis.

The students that I remember who transferred from Union High to Caroline High the first year of Freedom of Choice were Alphonso Jackson Jr., Nona McReynolds, Sylvia Johnson, myself. We all graduated together in 1968. I chose Caroline High because it was closer to me than Ladysmith High.

The first day, we rode the school bus with no problems that I remember. After that, there were problems. The children on the school bus would call us names and hit us. We would be fighting many afternoons getting off the bus. The bus driver was racist and not very helpful. She just ignored everything that was going on. The bus problems persisted the entire time I attended Caroline High.

During my senior year, as I approached the bus to get on, an elementary-aged child leaned out

the window, harked, and spat on me. I rushed on the bus, grabbed him by the neck, and choked him until the bus driver pulled me off him. The bus driver wanted to put me off the bus, but my mother met with the principal, and I was allowed to continue riding the bus. I don't remember having any problems after that.

I did not have problems in the classroom. Some students would make rude remarks. Most teachers were nice. I was a good student, and they were very supportive of me. Other teachers were racist. Eventually, I joined several clubs. I was a member of the band, choir, the debate club, the track team, and the basketball and softball teams. I made friends, but we did not socialize outside of school.

The assassination of MLK was a very lonely time for me. I heard many jokes and racist remarks at school during a time I mourned the loss of someone I admired and respected. I missed being in an environment where everyone felt the same about his death and comforted each other. Bobby Kennedy was assassinated during the time we were practicing for graduation. I remember a group of us leaving school and going to the beach.

When I first arrived there was no recognition of Negro History Week, but I do remember them celebrating Cat Week. I remember protesting Cat Week celebration, and by the time I graduated Negro History Week was a part of the school celebration.

I sacrificed my social life by attending Caroline High. I did not go to my junior or senior prom, go on a date, or have friends outside of school. I lost touch with some of my Union High friends after entering college.

After attending Caroline High, I realized most of my fears were unfounded. I was an honor student and able to compete with the students at Caroline High. I graduated third in my class. I also realized people were people. There were good students and bad students. There were good teachers and bad teachers. I think that by desegregating the school we helped to break down a lot of barriers and myths that each race had about the other. We laid the groundwork for the entire school system to be integrated without violence.

When I was looking at colleges my senior year, my mother wanted me to attend colleges like Mary Washington, University of Virginia. I felt I had done my part for the Civil Rights movement and wanted to be around Black people where I would be fostered in an environment which celebrated my Blackness and instilled in me that I was Black and much to be proud about. I am a graduate of Virginia Union University, a historically Black institution.

Looking back, I think the experience was necessary. It taught me that people are not defined by the color of their skin. We share humanity, and good or bad is based on one's character and integrity and not one's color. I learned to interact with White people, share the joys of victory and agony of defeat. It helped to dissolve the myths and stereotypes I had about White people. At times the journey was hard, but having completed it, I can now say it was a trip worth taking.

Beryl Jackson
Attended Union High from 1963 to 1965
Graduated from Caroline High in 1968

My husband [Albert T. McReynolds Jr.] and I talked about sending the children to the White schools when we first heard about Freedom of Choice. A lot of the parents were reluctant. He was from Washington, D.C., and thought it would be for the best. I was the holdout because I grew up in Caroline County and knew how prejudiced some people could be. It was not a problem for me because, as the old folks used to say, "We knew how to stay in our place."

Eventually, we decided to send all the children to White school except Michael. Michael had been promised a college scholarship by Aerospace. He was happy about the scholarship and going to college. Mrs. Dungee had worked so hard to help him get the scholarship. We decided he should stay at Union.

We had lived on military bases in Eta Jima, Japan, and Fort Knox, Kentucky, when my husband was in the Korean War. The military bases were integrated, and the children attended integrated dependent schools on the military base. Because they had already attended integrated schools, we thought it was going to be a nice transition.

Nona was the first girl to integrate Caroline High School; Brian "Kirk" also went there. Carla and Kevin went to Caroline Elementary. They had it rough. The younger children would tell what happened if asked, but the older children would keep it to themselves. Carla would not say anything, but if I asked what happened in school she would burst into tears and tell me what happened. She said the students made fun of her and would laugh at her. That would hurt me because Carla used to be so happy, easy going and loved all her teachers at Union Elementary.

The older children felt they could handle things. In the beginning, the students got physical with Nona. She did not tell me about it, but the principal did. One day I received a phone call from the principal [of Caroline High]. He was very upset and apologetic. It seems that when Nona was walking down the hall a group of four or five boys shoved her. She stabbed the boy closest to her with a lead pencil. A teacher saw what happened and told the principal. When the principal called me, he kept apologizing and saying it would not happen again. After that, Nona did not have any more problems.

Mr. Gibson was the coordinator for desegregation. He was a federal government official who was responsible for making sure the transition went well. In the first few months of school, he would call the house every school day after dinner time. He would say, "Mrs. McReynolds, I don't want to talk to you. I want to talk to the children." He would talk to each child to see how they were treated and how they were adapting.

I had mixed feelings when I saw how the children were being treated. They were comfortable at Union. I would talk to them about why what they were doing was important in the long term. The older children understood.

Looking back, I think it was worth it. Someone had to start integrating the schools. Now the children in Caroline County all get along very well and are happy. When I see how things are now, I realize it was all worth it.

Ivone Parker McReynolds
Mother of students who transferred from
Union High and Union Elementary to
Caroline High and Caroline Elementary in 1965

I attended Union High school in the 8th and 9th grades. The summer before the 10th grade, I tried out for the football team. The coach told me I was too small. I had a friend who had transferred to Caroline High the previous year, so I decided I would transfer to Caroline High so I could play football. I told my parents about my decision, and they supported me. They told me it would be a different environment, but I did not care. I just wanted to play sports. I contacted the Caroline High football coach, and he told me to come try out. I tried out and made the team.

I started at Caroline High in September 1966. I played on the football team. In the 10th grade, I did not start and played about half a game. I was a starter in the 11th grade. I played wide receiver on offense and defensive back on defense. In addition to playing football, I played basketball and ran track.

The three years I spent at Caroline High were a challenge for me because it was the first time I had been around Whites. I did not notice much difference between Union and Caroline High. Caroline had a better football field and track. The classrooms were about the same.

The Caroline teachers were not as caring as the teachers I had a Union High. The Union High teachers lived in my community and knew my parents. They really cared about me and wanted me to do well. The Caroline teachers just taught the class. I never experienced any problems at Caroline High. I rode the bus and no one bothered me. I did not have any problems with the teachers or the students. There were a few other Black students. We usually stayed together. In my senior year, I went to the junior-senior prom. I graduated in 1969.

William F. Garnett Jr.
Attended Union High from 1964 to 1966
Graduated from Caroline High in 1969

Integration:
The End of an Institution

The start of the 1969–1970 school year marked the end of Caroline County's segregated school system and the end of Union High School. The school was renamed Bowling Green Senior High School, and students were assigned to the school based on their geographic location, not race.

From most accounts, integration of the Caroline County School system was fairly uneventful. A few parents boycotted sending their children to Dawn Elementary, but there were no large protests or demonstrations.[91] Some parents established private academies to provide alternatives to public schools. Although these academies had an open admission policy, no Blacks applied.[92]

Although many of the Union High teachers remained at Bowling Green Senior High School, there were changes in the administrative staff. Principal George B. Ruffin was replaced and given the title of Assistant Superintendent in Charge of Pupil Services, a position with no responsibilities. He retired from the Caroline County School system in 1971. The assistant principal accepted an associate professor position at Virginia State College. His wife, Fraulein Coleman Lowe, a Union High counselor, accepted a position at the same college. Many of the Union High teachers remained at Bowling Green Senior High to teach, but others were sent to Ladysmith or Caroline High.

Members of the Black community felt torn about integration and the loss of Union High. On one hand, they were glad to see an end to segregation and being treated as second-class citizens. But on the other, they were sad to see the demise of an institution and many traditions that had played a vital role in their community for many generations. During segregation, there was a shared sense of responsibility for all children.

Adults nurtured and motivated children to strive for excellence, work to their fullest potential, and give back to their community. These values and expectations were the same at home, in school, and at church. After integration, this sense of togetherness was lost.

We knew integration was coming the next year. We were so happy we would get to graduate before the end of Union High. We call ourselves "The Last of the Best." The baccalaureate service was very emotional. That is when it hit us—that was the end of Union High, and we were the last graduating class.

Catherine Ferguson
Class of 1969

Integration did not bother the teachers. Many stayed at Union [renamed Bowling Green Senior High]. Only the administrators were impacted because they had too many principals since they were consolidating schools. They got rid of the Black principals. Mr. Ruffin became assistant superintendent on the Caroline County School Board. It was just a title—he had nothing to do.

I knew that they [the school board] would be getting rid of the Black administrators after integration. I decided to get additional education to be prepared. To avoid integrating their universities, the state of Virginia would pay the difference between the cost of attending the University of Virginia and an out-of-state school for Blacks wishing to obtain a degree not offered by a Black college in Virginia. The state of Virginia paid a portion of the cost for me to attend George Washington University. After school, I would drive to D.C. and take classes in the evenings and drive back to Caroline County after class. I received my master's and later my Ph.D. in 1969 from George Washington University.

When the county ruled the schools must integrate, I contacted Virginia State College to see if they needed someone with my experience. They did. I left the school system in 1969 and went to Virginia State, where I worked for 15 years. I was hired as an associate professor of education and faculty advisor to students who were writing their theses. I was also instrumental in developing the schools program in education administration and supervision. My wife, Fraulein Coleman Lowe, also went to Virginia State, where she became director of the University Counseling Center. She retired from the position in 1983. I retired in 1984, and we returned to Caroline County.

Dr. Walter E. Lowe
Industrial Arts Teacher
Assistant Principal
Coach

I will always be loyal to Union High. When I was at my cousin's graduation in 1960 (I was in the 1st grade), Mr. Ruffin was talking to my mother. He patted me on my head and said, "Young fella, it won't be long before you graduate from Union High." I did not get to graduate from Union High because of integration. I only attended Union High for the 8th and 9th grades. I was in the chorus, the band and was a bat boy for the baseball team. I played football in the 9th grade.

I wanted to stay a Union after integration. The power lines were used to determine the school boundaries. The students where I lived had to go to Ladysmith [formerly C. T. Smith]. We were better off at Union High. It was bigger than Ladysmith, had better clubs, a more robust curriculum (eg., commercial foods, barbering, masonry, etc.), better teachers and programs.

I was a member of the football team at Ladysmith. We had practice during the summer, so the Black and White students got to know each other. On the first day of practice, one boy name Reggie Prescott treated us nice and invited everyone to

his house to play basketball. He told us about the teachers and the school. When school started in September, all the football players were comfortable walking through the halls because of Reggie. He made the transition smooth.

There was a lot of change going on. I went along with the change, went with the flow. I did not have any problems at Ladysmith. I got along with everyone. I graduated from Ladysmith in 1972, but my heart belongs to Union High.

Arthur Sizer Jr.
Attended Union High 1967–1969
Graduated from Ladysmith High 1972

I really had mixed feelings [on learning Union High would no longer exist]. On one hand, I was sure that Blacks and Whites would get the same education. On the other hand, I was sad. I felt that what we had could never be duplicated in a different setting.

Dorothy Carter Black
Class of 1952

We knew that integration was coming. We talked about it at home and school. We had been taught so much pride in our school. There was a sense of pride to attend it. It did not matter that they changed the name of the school—to me it was still Union High.

We had a new principal, Mr. Hurt, but many of the old teachers were still there—Ms. Rucker, Ms. Luck, Ms. Banks, and Ms. Ragland. A new guidance counselor, Mrs. Brittle, replaced Ms. Lowe. When the school changed to Bowling Green High Senior School, it was not the same. Union High was like family—there was closeness. That was lost after the school changed. The teachers talked to the students differently. They were a lot more cautious. Before, if they had something to say to a student, they would say it in front of the whole class. After we became Bowling Green Senior High, they would take the student aside and say it to them privately. The students got along fine. It was a smooth transition.

When I got ready to graduate, I was disappointed that I was not graduating from Union High like the rest of my family. I felt like I was breaking a family tradition. My diploma said Bowling Green Senior High School instead of Union High.

Joyce Woolfolk Spencer
Attended Union High 1967–1969
Graduated from Bowling Green Senior High
School 1971

I was not concerned when integration came; I just continued to do the best I could. I felt everyone would be better off with integration. The Black students would have better opportunities with the White students.

Ola Luck
Librarian

After integration, I continued to teach at Bowling Green Senior High School. The teachers had to be very careful because everyone was watching what we did. Integration went better than I thought. A lot of my fears did not come true. The students got along, and some even became friends. I continued to teach at Caroline High School when the new one was built and retired in 1988.

Carolyn Bundy Johnson
Class of 1945
Mathematics Teacher

During the 1968–1969 school year we knew that integration was coming. I was not fearful or anything. Since I had taught at Caroline High, I had an idea of what the experience would be like. The mood at graduation was somewhat somber. We knew this was the end of an era and history was being made.

The next year, I was assigned to Bowling Green Senior High [formerly Union High]. Integration was relatively smooth. I had no problems. The administration treated me fairly, and I got along with the teachers and students. After we moved to the new Caroline High, the teachers would meet every Friday morning for a prayer service. We talked about ways we could do other activities together. Someone suggested we visit each other's churches. One of White teachers stated that we [the Black teachers] would not be welcomed at her church.

Some of the positive aspects of the Black community were lost after integration. For the most part, Black children were very respectful of adults. Children did not get involved in adult conversations and did not question authority; they knew their place. After integration, I did notice some of the Black children picked up the habits of some of the White children. They were less respectful, talked to adults like they were adults, and questioned authority. I took the kids on a field trip to the bank. Some of them were smoking in the back of the bus. When we got to the bank, some went out the emergency exit on the bus [instead of the front door]. I was not accustomed to students acting like that. Needless to say, we did not take many field trips after that.

There was a lot of pride at Union High. We sang the school song at all the games and activities. We were the Mighty Pointers and had a lot of school pride and camaraderie. All of that was lost after integration. We gained better educational opportunities after integration, but we lost a lot too.

Geneva Johnson Thompson
Class of 1963
Business Teacher

Legacy

Although Union High School no longer exists, it lives on in the hearts and memories of those who were privileged to be associated with the school. Union High alumni, family, and friends worked hard to ensure the historical significance of the school is not forgotten. On August 31, 1952, the Caroline Sunday School Union dedicated a plaque in the new school building to recognize and honor the early pioneers in the fight to provide educational opportunities to African American children in Caroline County, Virginia.[93] The plaque, which remains in the building today, has an inscription which reads:

Union High Commemorative Marker. PHOTOGRAPH BY MARION WOODFORK SIMMONS, JULY 24, 2010.

> This building is dedicated
> as a tribute to
> Rev. R. W. Young D.D. • Rev. A .P. Young B.D.• Rev. L. L. Davis   Deacon R. B. Fortune • Brother H. P. Latney
> For more than a half century these pioneers of private and public education labored beyond the call of duty and worked ceaselessly in upbuilding the religious, civil, and educational welfare of their country.
> Presented by The Caroline Baptist Sunday School Union
> Oliver W. Latney President

For several years after integration, the Union High building continued to be used as a school, first as Bowling Green Senior High School, then as Caroline Middle School. It was later used for gym classes by Bowling Green Primary School and

activities for the county's park and recreation department. It was later turned over to the county, which renovated the building and renamed it Caroline County Community Service Center. The building is now the home of the Caroline Library and other county offices.

In 1995, Dr. Walter Lowe, school board representative from the Mattaponi district, initiated efforts to recognize the significance of Union High. As a result of his efforts, the school board and the board of supervisors provide matching funds ($2,500 each) to obtain a historical marker for the former Union High site. A committee with representatives from the five magisterial districts was appointed to decide the best way to preserve the schools history.[94] The committee decided to purchase a memorial stone and created a collage to commemorate the historical significance of Union High school. The stone is located near the front of the building and contains the following inscription:

> Union High School
> 1903–1969
> Dedicated to the members of the African American Church Community who believed that "Knowledge is Power" and that the School is the Social Hub of the Community

The committee also successfully petitioned the board of supervisors to approve adding the words "Formerly Union High School" to the name on the front of the building.

Union High alumni remain connected through reunions and other social functions. In October 2010, more than 400 guests—graduates from the 1930s forward—attended an All Classes Reunion. Money from the reunions is used to endow the George B. Ruffin Scholarship Fund which provides college scholarships for children whose parents are Union High alumni.

The Union High History Project asked participants, "How would you like Union High to be remembered?" Their answers follow.

Union High was a good high school, with good teachers.
Susie Carter Quash
Class of 1947

Union High was a school where the success of the students came first and students felt safe. Teachers visited students' homes. Students studied hard and had many successes even though we did not have access to all of the supplements available to today's students. If a student was experiencing trouble, teachers were always available to offer assistance.
Irene Quash Fields
Class of 1947

Let not the legacy of Union High be entombed with the ruins of the buildings. But what WE, the students who walked the halls and studied in the class rooms have done to make society a better place for all mankind. Hail Union High, may your spirit live forever.
Daisy Jackson Thomas
Class of 1950

Union High was a community where people cared about each other—we were like family. They prepared us for life after high school by stimulating a thirst for knowledge.
Dorothy Samuels Vaughn
Class of 1950

Union High provided a cornerstone for the future. They gave us a solid foundation for a productive life and encouraged us to perform at our highest potential.
Evelyn Wright Thompson
Class of 1958

Caroline Community Service Center entrance. PHOTOGRAPH BY MARION WOODFORK SIMMONS, JULY 24, 2010.

Union High was a Virginia treasure where I was taught to always do my best, to take pride in whatever I did, and to respect differences in others. These memories would have little meaning without friends, especially the late Thelma Williams Jackson with whom I shared many happy days at Union and who was truly a good friend and best buddy for over 50 years.

Emma Samuel Vaughan
Class of 1950

Union High was a very good school, a great place to be. I don't think I would have done any better if I had gone to another school. It was like an oasis.

Dorothy Carter Black
Class of 1952

Union High was a good place where a lot of people got a good start. It gave us a basic education and taught us how to make a living. A lot of us achieved the American Dream (house, car, career, etc.).

Morton Upshaw
Class of 1953

Union High was a close-knit family where the teachers were genuinely interested in the children and their programs.

Jeanetta Rock Lee
Class of 1952
Secretary

Union High was a good place. The teachers were sincere and really cared about the students.

Aterita Baker Brown
Attended Union High from 1958 to 1961

We came together as one. Students and teachers cared about each other. The school taught us how to love and care about each other. We were like family.

Carolyn Jackson
Class of 1961

Union High was dedicated to academic achievement for all students. Education was taken very seriously. Students were thankful for the opportunity to go to the school. Union High provided students with the opportunity to reach their fullest potential.

Gladys Fitzhugh-Pemberton
Class of 1964

Union High was the central place where all Black children in the county went to school and got to know each other. It was a caring, student-centered school.

Patricia Sizer Adams
Class of 1964

Union High was a place where we received a good education that prepared us to be successful. We also had fun and made lots of lifelong friends.

Sherrillyn LaVerne Smith Silver
Class of 1965

Union gave me the foundation to become a good citizen. They taught us responsibility, character, and how to love your brother. It produced role models because the teachers were role models. Most of all, it gave us an education to compete on a national level.

William Brawner
Class of 1966

Union High was a very important cornerstone of the African American community. Not just for education but social and living too.

Paulette Sizer Davis
Class of 1968

Union High was an institution that provided the cornerstone of education for many students. It was a beacon of hope for students.

Beryl Jackson
Attended Union High from 1963 to 1965
Graduated from Caroline High in 1968

Union High prepared me for life by giving me the motivation to excel. They taught me, "You can do what you want to do but you must be responsible. If you fail, try again."

Calvin Taylor Sr.
Class of 1969

There was a lot of fellowship at Union High—it was a like a family. They instilled in students the struggle that took place so we could get an education and taught us to speak out against injustice. They helped us develop character and self-esteem. They helped sustain us in life.

They made us see and believe we were somebody, we were just as good as anybody else, we could compete against anyone. They taught us to be proud of who we were. They would say, "Don't think of yourself as coming from a small county school."

Catherine Ferguson
Class of 1969

Union High was a great institution and the cultural hub of the Black community in Caroline County, Virginia. It had good teachers with high morals.

Arthur Sizer Jr.
Attended Union High 1967–1969
Graduated from Ladysmith in 1972

I would like Union High to be remembered for its well-qualified teachers. It also served as the social hub of the community and will always be remembered by its Alma Mater "Dear Old Union High."

Clara Latney Hudson
Class of 1949

I want Union High School to be remembered as a warm and familiar, a soft place to land if you were falling—a place of hard choices but great rewards. I want it to be remembered as a stepping-off point to everything good in your future, a stepping-off point to personal and professional success. That's what that institution gave us. I want Union High to be remembered as a school that nurtured as well as educated.

Eleanor Thomas Hawkins
Class of 1965

I looked forward to going to school. It was a joyous time. I enjoyed being with my friends and teachers. Union High prepared me for life. I learned how to deal with obstacles in life. Union High's legacy is that it prepared me and others to become responsible adults.

Waverly Minor
Class of 1962

Union High was a family. Everybody knew everybody. The kids were everyone's kids. We had respect for the teachers, and they respected us. They cared about us. When we left home, we still were under parental care.

Geneva Johnson Thompson
Class of 1963
Business Teacher

Virginia's outstanding educational institution.
Oliver Washington
Class of 1953

Despite the adverse conditions of "separate and unequal" schools, Union High faculty members took personal interest in their students and were dedicated to providing a sound educational foundation. As a result, after completing high school, many students went on to receive undergraduate and graduate degrees in a variety of professions contributing to society. I am proud of the legacy of Union High School.

Evelyn Thomas Minor
Class of 1949

Union High was the backbone of the Black community in Caroline County. Everything was centered around the school. It was the glue that held the community together. When Union High closed, I felt a major part of history had been destroyed. I felt the school should have been a museum.

Joyce Woolfolk Spencer
Attended Union High 1967–1969
Graduated from Bowling Green Senior High School 1971

Union High School was an institution of higher learning for students, families, and the community. We cared for each other, and in our caring, we had a future for ourselves and our communities. We were really blessed. We can't ever forget the great people who were there for us all the time.

Judith Jones Budd
Class of 1953

It was one of the best schools in the area. I have very fond memories of Union High and my time there. Union High provided me with opportunities that I greatly appreciated. These opportunities helped form the foundation upon which I was able to learn and grow. I was able to carry these skills and life lessons with me into my professional career with the D.C. government, and I was able to advance largely because of what I was taught while attending Union High.

Cassandra Marie Davis
Brown
Class of 1950

I would like the world to know that Union High School was a very positive educational environment. There were very high standards set there. It was not a negative, nor an inferior

place where the leftovers were given to those "poor little Colored chillin." It was a place of dignity and grace. There were many property owners' children in that school. My paternal grandfather purchased our family property (29 acres) in the late 1800s. I have seen the deed, which shows how much he paid for it. Only a small portion of the school population qualified for the free-lunch program. The Union High school teachers were well-educated, and they deeply cared about their mission to educate in the tradition of W. E. B. DuBois and Booker T. Washington. Like them, our teachers carried out their mission. The proof is in their living legacy. We, the students who gradu-

In the 1950s, J. Shelby Guss (government teacher) wrote the words and Jewel A. Taylor (music teacher) composed the music for the Alma Mater.

ated from there, are the living proof. We have gotten advanced degrees and contributed to society on a world stage as doctors, lawyers, college professors, and military officers, to name a few. Union High graduates have done very well as mid- and upper-level managers and blue collar workers, who have raised families and have children and grandchildren who are professionals.

Williabel Jones Davis
Class of 1966

ALMA MATER

Dear Union High, you are a dream come true,

Born in the hearts of the men you've served.

And from your humble birth to your present age,

Your praises have always been heard.

Our love for thee will never waver;

Our loyalty will never sway.

Bind us close to thee, O'Union,

In this hour for thee we pray.

God bless our Alma Mater.

Bless old Union High.

She has been our sacred shelter,

In the many days gone by.

Protect her now and ever.

Let her banners fly.

She has been our inspiration,

Help us be her shining star.

Bless old Union High.

Help us love her forever,

Dear old Union High

School mascot The Pointer. SOURCE: *1967 UNION HIGH YEARBOOK*

Appendix A
Principal's Messages

Beginning in 1952, the principal wrote an annual message to the graduating class in the yearbook.
The message from each yearbook is included in this appendix.

MEMBERS OF THE GRADUATING CLASS OF 1952,

You are now about to leave us. Henceforth greater responsibilities and more exacting labors await you. For years your parents and your teachers have tried to direct you. You have been given all the advantages within their power to bestow. In your years of study you have been the recipient of intellectual benefits. In the years to come, it is your duty to give, rather than to receive, to share with others the bounty of your mind, and to make the world better and wiser for your having been in it.

Try to remember that it is not what man does which exalts him, but man would do.

Strive then, with faith in your power and trust in the infinite good, to do the tasks assigned to you, ever keeping sacred the integrity of your own mind, then you cannot hope too much.

Depend not on fortune but on conduct, for no man is free who is not master of himself. It is well said that: Command of one's self is the greatest empire a man can aspire unto. He who best governs himself is best suited to govern others.

[George Brown Ruffin]

1953

I congratulate you for completing your high school course at Union High School. As you now join the noble company of Union's sons and daughters, I trust that knowledge gained, advice received, and friendships experienced will fit you for further and even more exciting quests and discipline.

May you become even more punctual, accurate, and faithful as you face the test of life, which may be far sterner than those already experienced by you. The [acquirements] of a worthwhile education necessarily meant hard work, hours of grind,

consistency of purpose, and cheerful purposeful sacrifice gladly given. These constitute the legitimate price that every earnest student must pay.

Someone has said that success is best measured by the strength of opposition. Those who go to the summit of a mountain only when it can be reached by automobile will never feel the exhilaration of the climb of the cliff. Those who sail their boats over an eternally calm summer sea will never know what it means to master the storm.

Scores of Union's graduates have already made enviable records and contributions in their various walks of life. It is today that you become their intimate comrades and they welcome you into a fellowship made sacred by their devotion to the truth and the good life.

A sincere friend,
George Brown Ruffin

MEMBERS OF THE GRADUATING CLASS OF 1954,

I commend you for reaching this point in your preparation for life through sacrifice and labor. There are two ways to attain an important end—one is through force, and the other, through perseverance. Force falls to the lot of only the privileged few, but austere and sustained perseverance can be practiced by the most insignificant. Its silent power grows irresistible with time. Almost every good thing must be won, not by luck or accident but by honest toil.

Slumber not in the tents of the past, for the world is advancing. Advance with it! Use your gifts and training faithfully, and they will become enlarged. Practice what you know, and you shall attain higher knowledge. The grandest of all laws is the law of progressive development, for all that is human must retrograde if it does not advance.

Where we are is not as important as the direction in which we are moving.

Character is the foundation of all worthwhile success. A good heart, benevolent feelings, and a balanced mind lie at the foundation of character. Other things may come and go, but character is that which lives and abides within and is admired long after its possessor has left the earth. True worth is in being, not seeming—in doing each day that goes by, some little good—not in dreaming of great things to do.

Your obligations are plain and simple and consist of but three duties: your duty to God, which every man must feel, to your country, and to your neighbor, to do as you would be done by.

Numerous are the graduates of Union High School who have already found their places in making worthwhile contributions to society. May your becoming a part of this great family give to it added impetus and assurance to more noble achievements.

A sincere friend,
George Brown Ruffin

I CONGRATULATE YOU, MEMBERS OF THE GRADUATING CLASS OF 1955,

for having successfully completed a portion of your life's preparations—a step so necessary to advance-ment. The moral law of the universe is progress, and every generation that passes idly over the earth without adding to that progress remains uninscribed upon the register of humanity, and the succeeding generations trample its ashes to dust.

Virtue lies in the struggle and not in the prize. That which grows slowly endures. No road is too long to the man who advances deliberately and without undue haste, and no honors are too distant for the man who prepares himself for them with patience.

No man is free who cannot command himself. The most precious of all possessions is power over oneself, for he that hath not mastery over his inclinations, he that knows not how to resist the importunity of present pleasures for the sake of what reason tells him is fit to be done, is in danger of never being good for anything. The end of all

education is to make an individual good, to make him useful, to make him powerful in order that he may exert a helpful influence upon his fellow man.

A real life always lies in giving, never in receiving. A noble Jew named Jesus once let Himself be mastered by this theme. In so doing, He pioneered and occupied new spiritual ground. If we ignore His victory, I believe we ignore our destiny. Let us be dutiful to God and to our Country and to our fellow men.

Hundreds of Union High School Graduates are giving their best to humanity. Today I extend to you a cordial welcome to join this great family and to make the world better by your having lived in it.

A sincere friend,
George Brown Ruffin

IT IS WITH MUCH SINCERITY THAT I COMMEND EACH MEMBER OF THE CLASS OF 1956,

I trust that your knowledge gained and experiences had while attending this institution will aid you in becoming better citizens, that your quest for knowledge will not cease, that your character will be ever good, and your zeal to help fellowmen will be endless.

Remember that knowledge is not a couch whereon to rest a searching and restless spirit, nor a terrace for a wandering mind to walk upon, nor a sort of commanding ground for strife and contention. Instead, knowledge is ecstatic in enjoyment, perennial in fame, unlimited in space, and infinite in duration. In the performance of its sacred offices, it fears no danger, spares no expense, explores sea and land, contemplates the distant, comprehends the great, and ascends to the sublime. No place is too remote, no height is too exalted for its reach. However, knowledge without wisdom is folly, without kindness is fanaticism, and without religion is death.

Good character is human nature in its best form. It is moral order embodied in the individual. Men of character are not only the conscience of society, but in every well-governed state, they are its best motive power, for it is moral qualities which in the main rule the world. Other things may be deemed fortuitous; they may come and go, but character is that which lives and abides and is admired long after the possessor has left the earth.

The path of duty lies in what is near, and the best preparation for the future is the present well seen to and last duty well done. Be not daunted by difficulties, for the greater the obstacle, the more glory we receive in overcoming them. For the great high road of human welfare lies along the old highway of steadfastness and well doing, and they who are the most persistent and work in the truest spirit will invariably be the most successful.

The sons and daughters of Union High, your Alma Mater, are found in countless stations of duty and service over our state and nation. It is today that I welcome you into this great family, believing that your faith is eternal; for with faith in God we can endure all things and accomplish many.

A sincere friend,
George Brown Ruffin

IT GIVES ME MUCH SATISFACTION TO CONGRATULATE THE CLASS OF 1957 for having met the requirement for graduation at this institution. I am certain that you will not cease preparing yourselves to live worthwhile lives nor allow your quest for knowledge to wane. For knowledge always desires increase. It is like fire that must be kindled by some external agent, but it is comparatively worthless unless digested into practical wisdom and good judgment. It is the comfort of old age and makes men fit company for themselves.

Remember that life, however short, is made shorter by the loss of time, for time is the cradle of hope and the grave of ambition. It is the stern corrector of fools but the salutary counselor of the wise. It warns us with a voice that even the wisest discredit too long and that the silliest believe too late. Wisdom walks before it, opportunity with it, and repentance behind it. He that has made time his friend will have little to fear from his enemies, but he that has made it his enemy will have little to hope from his friends.

Hardships and opposition are the native soil of manhood and self-reliance. It is not ease but effort, not facility but difficulty that makes men. The acorn does not become an oak in a day, the ripened scholar is not made by a single lesson, and there are always months between the seed time and the harvest. For perseverance gives power to weakness and opens to poverty the world's wealth. It spreads fertility over the barren landscapes and bids the choicest fruits and flowers to spring up and flourish in the desert abode of thorns and briers.

You are obligated to use well your talents to bring about happiness, to help your neighbors, to serve your country in its needs with kindness and diligence in words and deeds, to think without confusion clearly, to act with honest motives purely, to love your fellow men sincerely, and to trust in God securely.

The illustrious sons and daughters of Union High School are many, their reputation and services are most valuable. It is you that we now invite to become members of this noble family. Trusting that you will be true to your Alma Mater, true to God, and true to all Mankind.

A Sincere Friend,
George Brown Ruffin

IT IS WITH MUCH PLEASURE THAT I CONGRATULATE EACH MEMBER OF THE GRADUATING CLASS OF 1958 for having completed the required courses and experiences for this achievement. It is my sincere hope that your efforts to grow in knowledge and to be of good character will not end here, that your faith will be excellent, and your eagerness to serve humanity will always be great.

There is always a need to grow in knowledge, for the more we know about our world and people about us, the better prepared we are to live the full and happy life. Our world is a[n] ever renewing world. Every day, with its new inventions and discoveries, new problems and new dangers, requires new vision and an increased stock of knowledge. The law of growth is as great as the universe and as old as time. The acorn teaches it; the oak exemplifies it. It is said to be gentle enough to color a rose and mighty enough to make a world. Finally, it may be described as God's beautiful law of evolution working not only in our bodies but shaping our minds and characters, as well as a force that makes things grow from weak to strong and from good to better everywhere.

Growth in good character is the greatest hope of the society of today. For good character is in all cases the fruit of personal exertion. It is not inherited, nor is it created by external advantages. It is the result of one's own endeavors. Character is made of vigorous and persistent resistance to evil tendencies. It is the fruit and reward of good principles manifested in a course of virtuous and honorable action.

Desirable character and knowledge well used can best be realized through eternal faith, for he who believes is strong, and he who doubts is weak. There is a limit to where intellect alone can travel and all the scholastic scaffolding falls as a ruined edifice if faith is lacking. Faith marches at the head of the train of progress. It is found beside the most refined life, the freest government, the noblest poetry, and purest humanity.

Remember that the best preparation for the future is the present well seen to and the last duty well done, for the path of duty lies in what is near, though men too often seek for it in what is remote. Your duty is clear and simple and consists of your obligations to God and to humanity.

Many the sons and daughters of Union High School who are rendering countless services in the various parts of our land and country. Today we invite you to join this great family, and may your doing so give to new vigor, strength, and greatness.

A sincere friend,
George Brown Ruffin

MEMBERS OF THE CLASS OF 1959, it is with much sincerity that I congratulate you for having reached this point in your life's preparation. This was done through sacrifice and toil, and I trust that you will ever have such austere and sustained perseverance to attain important goals, for its silent powers grow irresistible with time.

Remember that education is a continuing process and does not end with the mere acquisition of diplomas and degrees. The world is a scene of rapid changes where new knowledge and learning serves as an agency by means of which necessary adjustments and adaptations can be made to meet new situations and problems of our times.

"To live is not to live for one's self alone, for there is a destiny that makes us brothers, and none goes this way alone, for all that we send into the lives of others, comes back into our own.

Think truly and thy thoughts Shall the world's famine feed; live truly and thy life shall be a great and noble creed."

Today, we are asked to join the many sons and daughters of Union High School who render countless services throughout the country.

May your membership bring to your Alma Mater new vigor, greater perseverance, and countless achievements.

George Brown Ruffin

DEAR CLASS OF 1960,

The tree of knowledge is always full of fruit, but if there are never any windfalls, one must climb to reap the harvest. Your accomplishments in achieving this portion of your training shows that you wish to broaden your horizon. I sincerely hope that you will strive to participate in educational, recreational and religious activities which will take you far beyond activities of elementary needs.

I congratulate you, therefore, for this achievement and urge that you continue your pursuit for knowledge experiences that will make for you a fuller and richer life. All men do not live in a world of the same size. He who depends entirely upon his own unaided senses of sight, touch, and hearing lives in a tiny world as compared with the person who equips himself with a telescope, telephone, radio, and other scientific inventions. Perhaps the most important functions of educational institutions are to make man truly a human being and to give him a richer world in which to live.

However, no matter how exact a scientific

conclusion may seem, nor how definite a mathematical calculation, nor how firmly a moral principle seems to be established, man soon runs against the limits of his own ignorance. And unless he is mentally blind, he recognizes a huge realm of the unknown of which he knows practically nothing. Faced with the great uncertainty that lies beyond his proven knowledge, man requires faith in order to do this work. For faith gives meaning to human life, and religion develops and strengthens faith. He who believes is strong, but he who doubts is weak.

As you become sisters and brothers to the many illustrious sons and daughters of Union High School, may your deeds and consecrated services bring additional glory to your Alma Mater.

A sincere friend,
George B. Ruffin

CLASS OF 1961,

I welcome the opportunity to commend you for having successfully completed the required courses and experiences of this institution. This was possible only through constant attention to duty and hard work. As you enjoy the exercises and honors that accompany graduations, do not lose sight of the fact that educational growth is a lifetime adventure and does not end with the acquirement of diplomas and degrees.

Our world is an ever-renewing world. Daily and often hourly, new problems and new dangers, inventions, and discoveries require critical thinking and an increase in knowledge to make proper adjustments and adaptations. You are therefore challenged to use well your time and opportunities, for yesterday cannot be recalled, tomorrow cannot be reassured, and only today is thine. If you procrastinate, you will lose it.

Trying to stand still in a world that is always on a move will always lead to failure socially, politically, economically, and religiously. I trust that you will grow therefore in character, in learning, and in faith, remembering that growth has no end.

The number of sons and daughters of Union High School is consistently growing. Today we invite you to become members of this great family. May your joining this illustrious group bring to it additional glory and honor. And may you ever remain true to your God, true to your country, and true to your Alma Mater.

A sincere friend,
George Brown Ruffin

I WISH TO EXTEND MY CONGRATULATIONS TO THE CLASS OF 1962 for having met the requirements of our school curriculum. Your success is the result of conscientious toil, diligence and determination to achieve. I strongly urge that you do not pause here to rest upon the laurels gained thus far but that you will constantly seek excellence, for work and not repose is the destiny of man.

The popular cry for efficiency and modernity has become universal. The greatest purpose of intellectual cultivation is to give man a perfect knowledge and mastery of himself. It is only through constant study and experience of things that are moral, things that are scientific, and things that are Christian that we can expect to achieve excellence. This type of guided learning and deeds of consecrated service will enable you to probe new horizons, build worthwhile lives, homes, and communities.

To make the world better, lovelier, and happier is the noblest work of man. In the various parts of our country and even in foreign lands are found sons and daughters of dear old Union endeavouring to do just this. I am inviting you today to join this distinguished family and to ever strive to be true to your Alma Mater, true to your country, and true to God, the source of all love, light, and excellence.

A sincere friend,
George Brown Ruffin

IT IS WITH REAL PRIDE THAT I COMMEND YOU, THE CLASS OF 1963 for having reached this station in your preparation to meet the ever increasing challenges of life. It is now evident that you are living in an era in which the entire storehouse of human knowledge grows so rapidly that you must be prepared constantly to update your knowledge and skills if you are to function effectively as worthwhile citizens.

These changes make it not simply desirable but imperative that our education be considered a continuing lifelong process for all citizens. A continuing education becomes the growing and the harvest, for which formal schooling is only the planting and cultivation. This concept of education is becoming a vision of society in which not just schools but all its parts are concerned with helping individuals to fulfill themselves. This is the ideal of an educative society—one in which the people turn to the educated citizen for citizenship, tolerant but not indifferent, loyal but not bigoted, aggressive but not conceited, and alert but not alarmed.

However, there is a limit to where knowledge and intellect can travel, and all its scholastic scaffolding falls as a ruined edifice if faith is lacking. For faith marches at the head of the train of progress and is found beside the most refined life, the freest government, and the noblest poetry and purest humanity.

In this seventh decade of the Twentieth Century, you can find many sons and daughters of Dear Union High over the broad lands and country rendering countless services to their fellow men. As you graduate, you become sisters and brothers to the members of this illustrious family. May your doing so be accompanied with new vigor and greatness.

A sincere friend,
George Brown Ruffin

IT IS WITH MUCH SINCERITY THAT I COMMEND EACH MEMBER OF THE CLASS OF 1964 for having made this important beginning in the procurement of an education, for the history of mankind demonstrates without doubt that the advancement of a people is almost in direct proportion with the availability and the recognition of the importance of education and understanding of the world about them.

We are brought face to face with the new demands of living in a world that is changing so rapidly that the solution to many human problems are not applicable long enough to be transmitted from one generation to the next. Consequently, it behooves all of us to continually search for new truths and means to solve them.

Adequate knowledge only is indispensable for it is ecstatic in enjoyment, perennial in fame, unlimited in space, and infinite in duration. In the performance of its sacred office, it fears no danger, contemplates the distant, comprehends the great, and ascends to the sublime. No place is too remote, no height is too exalted for it to reach. However, knowledge without wisdom is folly, without kindness is fanaticism, and without religion is death.

May we ever remember that good character is human nature in its best form. Other things may be deemed fortuitous, they may come and go, but character is that which lives and abides and is loved long after the possessor has left this earth. Finally, be not daunted by difficulties for greater the challenge, greater still is the triumph.

Throughout our land and country and even abroad are found sons and daughters of dear Union High School, it is today that I invite you to join this illustrious family. May you ever be loyal and true to your Alma Mater, to your country, and to your God.

A sincere friend,
George Brown Ruffin

SENIORS OF 1965,

The journey through life itself is but the constant seeking after knowledge. The road ahead is full of adventures and opportunities. I congratulate you, therefore, for having reached this point in preparation for the challenges of the future. For today is not yesterday, and rapidity of change is the atmosphere in which you must live.

It is one thing to live in a world in which change is an exceptional situation amid the normalcy of a stable continuity of patterns of living, but it is quite a different thing to live in a world where change is normal and stable patterns do not exist. This new world of rapid innovations is not a disorderly world. The basis of its order, however, is not that things will stay as they have been but that disarrangements have continuity and are related to consequences which can be depended upon. Nor is this an insecure world, for its security is based not on one's confidence that he can understand the changes that will take place and that he has the knowledge and capacity to take advantage of the changes with the resources at hand.

I am asking you, then, to ever seek to grow in knowledge, usefulness, and faith, remembering that growth has no end and that all that is human must retrograde if it does not advance.

As you become daughters and sons of Union High, joining the great family of illustrious citizens which are found in various parts of the world rendering useful services, may your noble deeds and consecrated services bring additional glory to your Alma Mater.

Sincerely yours,
George B. Ruffin

MEMBERS OF CLASS OF 1966,

It can be said that time passes not from year to year, but from season to season. The four seasons which we know so well are monuments to a timeless year. However, unmistakable evidences are left behind. For the fullness of the ever-changing earth is witness to the chronicle. Leaves turn to a russet splendor and fall helplessly to the ground. A white mantle of snow covers the barren fields. Leaves grow green anew, later to be nurtured by the returning sun, thereby completing the cycle of time into small units, and the future of the mortals who pass into the midst of it is uncertain.

You who now depart from Union enter a season of external peace but of seething turmoil. It is customary for principals to remind their graduates of stumbling blocks, but we must remember that stumbling blocks have been placed there by men alone and only men can move them. You are being graduated into an ever-changing life whose varied phases are parallel of the earth's seasons. Just as the earth undergoes its metamorphosis, so will you, the graduates of '66, experience yours. As seasons change, so will your lives change, as each season marks the earth with its green, white, or russet personality, so will your lives alter and illuminate the future of mankind.

Let us remember that to make the world bet-

ter, lovelier, and happier is the noblest work of man. As you become sons and daughters of dear Union High, I trust that your contributions and deeds be ever glorious; and that you will ever remain true to your alma mater, to your fellow man, and true to your God.

Your sincere friend,
George Brown Ruffin

MEMBERS OF THE CLASS OF 1967,

I congratulate you for having reached this stage in your intellectual advancement. Education is indeed today a moral, economic, and social equipment for living in a world that is continually being renovated by new findings, new aspirations, and needs.

The winds of change are blowing over our society, and if we are indifferent to them, we may find too late that this wind has become a destructive hurricane. Our environment and the stupendous growth of knowledge is in such seething flux that the struggle for survival is more arduous than ever before. Consequently, you must possess a profound sense of values and courageously defend them, be able to discriminate between the significant and the trivial, between that which has beauty and integrity and that which is cheap and shoddy.

It is urgent, therefore, for you to make every effort, honestly and objectively, not only to understand the nature of the problems of our society but to comprehend compassionately the differences that separate it from others. It is your responsibility to try to make the world still better, to mitigate the hazards and shortcomings of our modern life and at the same time take pride in what modern civilization has wrought. You must face the world with quiet courage, determination, and above all with hope and faith.

A sincere friend,
George B. Ruffin

CLASS OF 1968,

I congratulate you for your successful beginning in your effort to cross the bridge between unpreparedness and preparedness, for bridges connect. They enable people to move from height to height, and to reach a chosen destination. Figuratively, we need a bridge between us and our aspirations, between ourselves and our acquaintances, between people and their leaders, and between nation and nation. These bridges lead from fear, suspicion, and distrust to faith and confidence. We must build such bridges, and each of us must learn how to build his own.

You who are graduating are crossing the bridge between adolescence and maturity. Commencement makes you a freshman again—a freshman adult. Now you must scan the map of life and select a destination. You want to "get somewhere in life," and you must travel the road that bridges the chasms of discouragement and doubt. Remember always that competence comes from the desire to possess it, but it is the pressure that you put on yourself which measures all that you accomplish.

A good bridge depends for strength on its design, its components, and its craftsmanship. The design is your plan of life, the components are knowledge, compassion, sincerity, and integrity while the quality of workmanship depends on you.

Build a bridge to your life's ambition. Be sure that there is a bridge to the people you meet. Join others in building a bridge between America and the other Nations of the World.

One more thing, when your bridge is built, CROSS IT.

Your sincere friend,
G. B. Ruffin

CLASS OF 1969,

I write this message with feelings difficult to describe and almost impossible to analyze. I am moved by the knowledge that our Commencement Exercises today not only finish the 5 years you have spent at Union, but also they signal the end of the 65th year of our beloved institution.

Your years at Union as members of the class of 1969 have been for you perhaps the most important ones of your life and will increasingly be so evaluated by you. They have been, I am sure, fleeting years for you as they have for me.

For you who graduate today, this is truly a commencement, a beginning. For each of you, a career now beckons as you plan the life you choose to build. Your decisions, if still uncertain, must now be made as to the contributions you will make to a nation and to a society in which the need for men of courage and conviction, of integrity and leadership, is more imperative, indeed, more crucial, than ever before in our history. The need for the removal of the inequities of our society and for the improvement of the world can best be brought about through the leadership of educated men who posses a background of the past, who understand he present, who plan wisely for a constructive movement toward a better future.

Today as you become sons and daughters of the great family of Unionites, may your loyalty to your Alma Mater, to your country, and to your God ever be strong.

A friend,
George Brown Ruffin

Appendix B
Historical Background

At the end of the Civil War, Negroes were technically no longer enslaved, but they had virtually no tools to become self-sufficient. During slavery, they had been denied education and never compensated for their work, so they were illiterate and impoverished through no fault of their own.

The newly freed Negroes were eager to become self-reliant, productive members of society. Education was seen as the key to a better life, and the newly freed slaves were eager to learn. Many organizations such as the Freedman's Bureau, missionary groups, and other benevolent societies from the North worked to establish schools to provide Negroes with a rudimentary education.

In the years immediately after the Civil War, several amendments to the Constitution were passed to ensure Negroes were given the rights of full American citizens. The Thirteenth Amendment abolished slavery and involuntary servitude. The Fourteenth Amendment granted citizenship to all people born or naturalized in the United States and guaranteed all citizens due process and equal protection. The Fifteenth Amendment gave Negro males 21 years old and older the right to vote. Many Whites believed Negroes were inferior and should be treated accordingly. Many Southern states passed legislation, which came to be known as Jim Crow laws, that

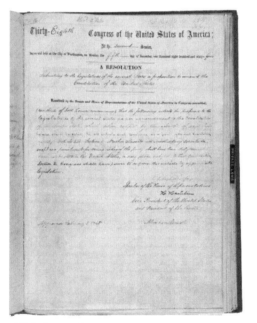

13th Amendment to the U.S. Constitution: Abolition of Slavery.
Source: The U.S. National Archives and Records Administration

created a system of segregation in which Negroes were denied access to all public facilities, services, and opportunities.[95]

In 1896, the Jim Crow laws were tested in the Supreme Court case of Plessey vs. Ferguson in which Homer Plessey, a Negro, appealed his conviction for breaking the Louisiana segregation laws by riding in a White-only railcar. The Supreme Court ruled that segregation was legal as long as the facilities were equal. This decision legalized the system of segregation put in place by the Jim Crow laws.

For several decades, America operated under the separate-but-equal doctrine.

In reality, society was separate but far from equal. Facilities provided for Negroes were usually inferior to those provided for Whites. And Negroes were subject to a number of social, economic, and educational disadvantages. In response to this system of segregation, Negroes established their own schools, businesses, and organizations.

Members of the Negro community saw education as the tool that would provide future generations with a better life. They pooled their resources to build one- and two-room school houses. Education in the rural south, especially for Negroes, faced ill-constructed, sparsely furnished facilities and poorly trained teachers.

Many White philanthropists established foundations and organizations to provide educational opportunities for Negroes in the south. John F. Slater, a manufacturer from Norwich, Connecticut, left $1 million in his will to be used to develop educational facilities for Negroes, and his estate founded the John F. Slater Fund in 1882. Before 1911, most resources were used to support Negro colleges. In 1911, Slater Fund Administrator Dr. James H. Dillard shifted the focus to establishing secondary schools in the public county and parish school systems. The goal was to establish one quality school in each county, called a county training school, that would serve as a public training school for teachers to address the problem of a shortage of qualified teachers in rural Negro schools.

Recipients of Slater Fund grants were required to meet certain prerequisites designed to make public authorities responsible for providing secondary educational facilities for Negroes in rural schools and raising the standards of the facilities. To receive a Slater Grant, the state, county, or district had to own the school property; the school had to be part of the public school system; no less than $750 had to be appropriated for salaries from public funds raised by state, county, or district taxation; and teaching had to extend through the 8th grade with the intention of adding at least two year. as soon as it was possible to do so.[96] In 1917, Julius Rosenwald, president of Sears and Roebuck, incorporated the Julius Rosenwald Fund to provide resources for building schools in rural Negro communities. The fund was designed to encourage communities and governments to take responsibility for needed programs and services for Negro children. Therefore, members of the community were required to raise money and provide the labor for construct-

ing a new school, and the state and local government had to agree to maintain the school as part of the public school system.

John D. Rockefeller organized the General Education Board (GEB) in 1902 to administer funds to promote education in the South.

Anna T. Jeanes, a Quaker from Philadelphia, left $1 million in her will to be used for improving small rural Negro schools. Her estate established the Negro Rural School Fund, Anna T. Jeanes Foundation (better known as The Jeanes Fund). Money from this fund was used to pay the salaries of industrial supervisors (better known as Jeanes Supervisors or Jeanes Agents). Jeanes Agents traveled across the rural South and worked with teachers at the local schools to improve the quality of education and the communities that the schools served.

There was much debate as to the best way to educate Negroes. Many philanthropists believed industrial education was the best form of education for Negro students because it would teach them to perform a trade that would allow them to become self-sufficient. Many people, especially those in the Negro community, felt industrial education did not prepare students for entry into higher education and prepared them only for menial jobs. But many Negro communities used the industrial education system to receive funds from philanthropic organizations for better facilities and funding for their schools. The curriculum consisted of both industrial classes such as domestic science and industrial arts and academic courses such as foreign language. Schools often held industrial exhibits and invited private fund representatives, White local residents, and state officials. The events allowed students to demonstrate what they had learned in hopes of increasing school funding.

SOURCE: *RUTHERFORD BIRCHARD HAYES, MEMORIAL OF JOHN F. SLATER, OF NORWICH, CONNECTICUT, 1815–1884 (UNIVERSITY PRESS: 1885)*

During the era of segregation, many Whites became concerned with racial purity. In March 1924, the Virginia General Assembly passed the Racial Integrity Act, which divided society into two racial categories: White and Colored. Virginia already had an anti-miscegenation law that banned interracial marriages. The act went a step further to make it a crime for White persons and non-White persons to marry.

The Racial Integrity Act defined race by the one-drop rule, which stated a person with any African or Indian ancestry should be classified as Colored. The act was later amended with the "Pocahontas exception," which stated a person could be considered White even if he or she had as much as one-sixteenth Indian ancestry. This exception was put in place because many influential First Families of Virginia claimed to be descendants of Pocahontas and would have been classified as Colored or non-White under the original classification system.

In 1909, an interracial group of people formed the National Association for the Advancement of Colored People (NAACP) to promote equal citizenship rights for all Americans. The NAACP used the court system to fight for equality. Most NAACP lawyers were protégés of Charles "Charlie" Houston and Howard University's Law School. A lawyer and the vice dean of Howard University Law School, Houston transformed the law school from an unaccredited night program to a well-respected, full-time accredited program.

Houston believed the role of a lawyer was to be a social engineer who worked within the legal system to fight for equality. He felt to be effective, a lawyer must understand the Constitution and

know how to use it to better the living conditions of underprivileged citizens. Under Houston's direction, Howard Law School became the training ground for Negro lawyers who led the fight to dismantle legal discrimination in America. Thurgood Marshall, lawyer for the landmark Brown v. Board of Education court case and the first Black Supreme Court Justice, is one of Houston's most notable students. But there are many other NAACP lawyers who worked diligently to end discrimination in America.

SOURCE: LIBRARY OF CONGRESS

Starting in the 1930s, the NAACP filed a series of lawsuits to make Negro schools equal with White schools and eventually abolish segregation in public education. The NAACP often appealed these cases all the way to the Supreme Court, which resulted in several landmark decisions that eventually ended school segregation in America.

In the mid 1930s, the NAACP took steps to force Southern states to provide equal access to graduate and professional schools. Alice C. Jackson was a part of this movement. In August 1935, she applied for admission to the University of Virginia graduate school and was denied admission. Her application was rejected, and school officials refused to explain why. The NAACP eventually decided not to pursue the case in court, but the threat of such a court case led many states to establish programs to provide Negroes with access to higher education facilities without building the facilities in their states. In 1936, the Virginia General Assembly passed the Dovell Act, which provided funds equal to the additional amount of tuition and travel expenses required for a Negro student to attend an out-of-state graduate or professional school offering a similar course of study.

In the late 1930s, the NAACP took up a case to challenge the unequal pay scales for Negro and White teachers. Aline Black, a high school teacher in Norfolk, Virginia, agreed to be the plaintiff in the fight for pay equality. On October 27, 1938, a petition was filed on her behalf with the Norfolk board of education asking them to adopt and enforce a pay scale that would bring her salary on par with White teachers of the same qualifications. The local court dismissed her request, and before the case could be appealed to the Virginia Supreme Court, the school board declined to renew her contract. She moved to New York.

Melvin Alston, president of the Norfolk Teachers Association, agreed to be a plaintiff in a new lawsuit. The case *Alston vs. School Board of the City of Norfolk* was ultimately taken to the U.S. Supreme Court, who denied the school board's appeal. In 1940, the Supreme Court ruled it was illegal to pay teachers with the same qualifications different salaries based on their race or color.

In the 1950s, under the leadership of the NAACP, parents in various locations filed lawsuits against the school board to bring an end to school segregation. One case was *Brown v. the Board of Education of Topeka Kansas*. The case ultimately reached the Supreme Court, where it was combined with four other cases: *Briggs v. Elliott* (filed in South Carolina), *Davis v. County School Board of Prince Edward County* (filed in Virginia), *Gebhart v. Belton* (filed in Delaware), and *Bolling v. Sharpe* (filed in Washington, D.C.). In 1954, the Supreme Court ruled that school segregation was unconstitutional and overturned the *Plessy v. Fer-*

guson decision of 1896, which allowed state-sponsored segregation.

In response to the Supreme Court ruling on *Brown vs. the Board of Education of Topeka Kansas*, many Southern states organized the movement known as Massive Resistance, in which a series of state laws were passed to prevent school integration. During this movement, Pupil Placement Boards were created to assign students to particular schools. Tuition grants were provided to students whose parents did not want them to attend integrated schools. State governments also had the power to deny funds to and close schools attempting to integrate.

Eventually, the U.S. Supreme Court ruled that Massive Resistance was unconstitutional. States then put in place Freedom of Choice programs in which families and students could choose to attend any public schools regardless of their race. But these programs did little to desegregate public schools.

On July 2, 1964, President Lyndon B. Johnson signed The Civil Rights Act of 1964 into law. Title VI of the Civil Rights Act of 1964 and the Elementary and Secondary Education Act of 1965 denied federal funds to schools that resisted integration. To obtain financial assistance from the Department of Health, Education, and Human Services, school boards were required to sign an Assurance of Compliance Pledge stating they would comply with the Civil Rights Act of 1964. Because federal funding made up a huge portion of the school board budgets, schools boards slowly began to institute plans to integrate their school systems. Segregation in other aspects of life in America began to be eliminated as well.

Appendix C
Union High History Project Participants

Ms. Patricia Sizer Adams, Student

Ms. Lottie Turner Armstead, Student

Ms. Norma Guss Bell, Student and Secretary

Mr. Herbert Beverly, Student

Mr. Reginald Arthur Beverly, Student and Teacher

Ms. Dorothy Carter Black, Student

Mr. Lloyd Boxley Jr., Son of Mr. Lloyd and Ms. Pauline Boxley (Teachers)

Ms. Pauline Shelton Boxley, Substitute Teacher and Wife of Mr. Lloyd Boxley (Teacher)

Mr. William Brawner, Student

Ms. Florence Coleman Bryant, Student

Ms. Yvonne Woolfolk Britton, Student

Ms. Aterita Baker Brown, Student

Ms. Cassandra Marie Davis Brown, Student

Mr. Douglas Hayes Buchanan Sr., Grandson of Mr. George Hayes Buchanan (Principal)

Mr. Mark Buchanan, Grandson of Mr. George Hayes Buchanan (Principal)

Ms. Judith U. Budd, Student

Ms. Diane Boxley Burnett, Daughter of Mr. Lloyd and Ms. Pauline Boxley (Teachers)

Ms. Ercelle Deyo Byrd, Student

Ms. Laverne Bates Carter, Student

Mr. Wesley T. Carter, Husband of Ms. Louise Byrd Carter (Teacher)

Ms. Joyce Byrd Cofield, Student

Ms. Lucille Howard Coleman, Student

Ms. Vivian Garnett Coleman, Student

Ms. Beulah Collins, Student

Ms. Joyce "Judy" Crump, Student

Ms. Paulette Sizer Davis, Student

Mr. Thomas Davis, Student

Ms. Williabel Jones Davis, Student

Mr. Boyd Deyo, Student

Rev. Joseph Dobbins, Student

Ms. Carolyn Garnett Epps, Student

Ms. Janie Anderson Edwards, Student

Ms. Catherine Ferguson, Student

Ms. Gladys Rich Ferguson, Student

Ms. Irene Quash Fields, Student

Mr. Bernard Freeman, Student

Ms. Vernelle Bates Frenzley, Student

Ms. Fannie Saunders Garnett, Student

Mr. William Garnett Jr., Student

Ms. Katrina Beverly Gill, Student

Mr. Charles Gray, Student

Mr. Rudolph Gray, Student

Mr. J. Shelby Guss, Student, Teacher

Ms. Nina Woolfolk Harley, Student

Ms. Clara Sizer Harris, Student

Ms. Regena Green Harris, Student

Ms. Lavern Baylor Gwathmey, Student

Ms. Eleanor Thomas Hawkins, Student

Ms. Clara Latney Hudson, Student

Mr. Arthur Jackson, Student

Ms. Beryl Jackson, Student

Ms. Carolyn M. Jackson, Student

Ms. Dorothy Samuels Jackson, Student

Mr. Jesse C. Jackson, Student

Ms. Marguerite Davis Jackson, Student, Teacher, Guidance Counselor, Granddaughter of Rev. Liston Leander Davis (Principal)

Ms. Mary Jeter, Student

Ms. Carolyn Bundy Johnson, Student and Teacher

Mr. Elmer D. Johnson, Student

Mr. James M. Johnson, Student

Mr. Stanley O. Jones, Student

Ms. Virginia Gray Latney, Student

Mr. Oliver Latney Jr., Student

Ms. Jeanetta Rock Lee, Student, Secretary, and Wife of Mr. Christopher C. Lee (Teacher)

Ms. Nancie Gray Lee, Student

Ms. Brenda Lockley, Daughter of Ms. Annie Maud Williams (student)

Dr. Walter E. Lowe, Teacher, Coach, and Assistant Principal

Ms. Ola R. Luck, Librarian

Ms. Nona McReynolds McLean, Student

Ms. Ivone Parker McReynolds, Student

Ms. Alma Thomas Mickens, Student

Ms. Vergie L. Miller, Student

Ms. Evelyn Thomas Minor, Student

Mr. Waverly Minor, Student

Mr. John Monte, Jr., Student

Ms. Bert Twiggs Nichols, Student

Mr. Kenneth Paige, Grandson of Ms. Ida Paige (student)

Ms. Margie L. Peatross, Student

Ms. Gladys Fitzhugh-Pemberton, Student

Ms. Mary Tillman Price, Student

Ms. Claudia Beverly Rollins, Student and Teacher

Ms. Rosa Bell Courtney Quash, Student

Ms. Susie Carter Quash, Student

Ms. Evelyn P. Ragland, Student

Ms. Gloria Woodfolk Reynolds, Student

Ms. Lorenza Young Robinson, Teacher

Ms. Barbara Jones Rock, Student

Ms. Florence Lee Rhue, Student

Ms. Kate Hutchinson Samuels, Student and Cafeteria Worker

Ms. Carrie Myers Saunders, Student

Ms. Sherrillyn LaVerne Smith Silver, Student

Mr. Arthur R. Sizer Jr., Student

Ms. Lillian Richardson Sizer, Student

Ms. Joyce Woolfolk Spencer, Student

Mr. Calvin Taylor Sr., Student

Mr. James Taylor, Student

Ms. Daisy Jackson Thomas, Student

Mr. Warren Thomas, Student

Ms. Evelyn Wright Thompson, Student

Ms. Geneva Johnson Thompson, Student and Teacher

Ms. Anna Marie Gray Thornton, Student

Ms. Jacqueline Rock Smith, Student

Ms. Blonnie Tipton, Teacher

Ms. Shirley Johnson Twiggs, Student

Ms. Shirley Vernelle Twiggs, Student

Ms. Vera Twiggs Underwood, Student

Mr. Morton Upshaw, Student

Ms. Emma Samuel Vaughn, Student

Ms. Blanche Lomax Washington, Student

Mr. Marshall E. Washington, Student

Mr. Oliver D. Washington, Student

Mr. Charles Woodfork, Student

Mr. Rogers Woolfolk, Student

Ms. Louise Boone Young, Student

Rev.. Walter Young, Student and Teacher

Notes

1   Caroline County Circuit Court, Deed Book 67:158, Bowling Green, Virginia.

2   Rev. R. W. Young, *The Educational Journal* Vol 1. (Jan. 1904): 1.

3   Young, 1.

4   Lester F. Russell, *Black Baptist Secondary Schools in Virginia, 1887–1957: A Study in Black History* (Metuchen, N.J.: Scarecrow Press, 1981): 85.

5   Caroline County Circuit Court, Deed Book 67:140

6   Russell,129

7   Caroline County Circuit Court, Deed Book 69:7.

8   Russell, 129.

9   Bowling Green Industrial Academy, Catalogue, Bowling Green, Virginia: Bowling Green Industrial Academy, 1905–1906, , 3. Many sources erroneously state the school was originally named Champlain and Bowling Green Industrial Academy and dropped Champlain from the name after the first year. The original source of this erroneous information is probably *A History of Caroline County, Virginia* by Marshall Wingfield. *The Educational Journal* published in January 1903 by The Bowling Green Industrial Academy and edited by Rev. L. L. Davis indicates after his graduation from Hampton Normal and Industrial Institute (now Hampton University) in 1888, Rev. Davis was put in charge of a grade school in Champlain, Virginia, which developed into a secondary school called Champlain Industrial High School. Rev. Davis resigned his position from the Champlain school in 1903 when he accepted the principal position at Bowling Green Industrial Academy.

10   *The Educational Journal,* op. cit.

11   Second Annual Report of the State Corporation Commission for Virginia for the Year Ending December 31, 1904, 134.

12   Certificate of Incorporation of Bowling Green Industrial Academy , State Corporation Commission, Charter Book 54, 223.

13   Certificate of Incorporation of Bowling Green Industrial Academy, 224.

14   Caroline County Circuit Court, Deed Book 71:373.

15   Caroline County Circuit Court, Deed Book 76:66.

16   *The Educational Journal,* op. cit.

17   Bowling Green Industrial Academy, 4.

18   Upton's tactics are a series of drill techniques that are used in the military.

19   Bowling Green Industrial Academy,11.

20   Report of the Commissioner of Education for the Year Ended June 30, 1912 Volume II,590.

21   Report of the Commissioner of Education for the Year Ended June 30, 1912Volume II, 590.

22   "Zealous Worker for Education," *The Afro American Ledger,* 11 July 1914.

23   *The Southern Workman* Volume XLIII (January through September 1914): 492. Caroline County Circuit Court, Deed Book, Deed Book 84:607.

24   State Board of Education, *Annual Report of the Superintendent of Public Instruction of the Commonwealth of Virginia, School Year 1918–1919 and 1919–1920*. Richmond, Virginia: Division of Purchase and Printing, 1920,124.

25   U.S. Department of the Interior, Bureau of Education, *Negro Education: A Study of the Private and Higher Schools for Colored People in the United States*, Bulletin, 1916, No.39, Vol. II, Washington, DC: U.S. Government Printing Office, 1917, http://books.google.com/ (accessed January 29, 2009), 620.

26   Fisk University Rosenwald Fund Card File Database (http://rosenwald.fisk.edu/).

27   Russell, 131.

28   State Board of Education, *Annual Report of the Superintendent of Public Instruction of the Commonwealth of Virginia, School Year 1928–1929*. Richmond, Virginia: State Board of Education, 1929, 48. Various sources have different dates for when the school became an accredited high school. This confusion may because of the way high schools were accredited. A high school applying for accreditation from the Virginia State Board of Education for the first time was obliged to maintain the minimum requirements for accreditation for at least one year before being placed on the state's list of accredited schools.

29   Russell, 131.

30   Gilbert C. Battle Jr., notes from Caroline County Public Schools School Board Meeting Notes, June 3, 1929.

31   State Board of Education, *Annual Report of the Superintendent of Public Instruction of the Commonwealth of Virginia, School Year 1929–1930*. Richmond, Virginia.: State Board of Education, 1930, 54

32   State Board of Education, *Annual Report of the Superintendent of Public Instruction of the Commonwealth of Virginia, School Year 1930–1931*. Richmond, Virginia: State Board of Education, 1931, 30.

33   Union High School, Catalogue. Bowling Green, Virginia: Union High School, 1930–1931, 5.

34   State Board of Education, 1929–1930, 55.

35   Ibid.

36   George B. Ruffin, "Accreditation," *The Pointer Review* (June 1967): 4.

37   State Board of Education, 1930–1931, 172.

38   Caroline County Public Schools, School Board Meeting Notes, March 7, 1938.

39   Caroline County Public Schools, School Board Meeting Notes, January 6, 1941.

40   Caroline County Public Schools, School Board Meeting Notes, March 6, 1942.

41   "Retired Caroline teacher wins Va. State alumni   award." *Free Lance Star*, June 4, 1980, 24

42   Will Schermerhorn, "Lloyd Boxley–Retiring after 37 years." *Caroline Progress*, June 6, 1984, 12.

43   This unofficial list of Union High faculty was compiled from information obtained from Union High Yearbooks, 1950–1969.

44   "Two 'Indians' Are Convicted Refused Designation as Colored for Army." *Baltimore Afro-American* [Baltimore] 1 Aug. 1944: 1–2. Google News. Web. 2 Apr. 2010.

45   Caroline County Public Schools, School Board Meeting Notes, July 6, 1954.

46   Caroline County Public Schools, School Board Meeting Notes, May 6, 1963.

47   Caroline County Public Schools, School Board Meeting Notes, July 1, 1963.

48   Caroline County Public Schools, School Board Meeting Notes, August 5, 1963, August 19, 1963.

49   Union High Class of 1950 Year Book, Class History.

50   State Board of Education, *Annual Report of the Superintendent of Public Instruction of the Commonwealth of Virginia, School Year 1949–1950*. Richmond, Virginia: State Board of Education, 1950, 41.

51   Florence C. Bryant, , *Memoirs of a County Girl* (New York, New York: Vantage Press, 1988), 110–111.

52   In the 1940's, many citizens of Caroline County were required to relocate when the federal government purchased approximately 60,000 acres of land in the Bowling Green area in order to establish a military reservation – named AP Hill - to be used as a training facility. Several communities ceased to exist after homes, churches, schools and other buildings were demolished and graves relocated to other cemeteries.

53   Rob Hedelt. "A Different Kind of Graduate." *Free Lance Star*. 24 Apr. 1979: 1+. *Free Lance Star*. Google News. Web. 26 June 2010.

54   Caroline County Public Schools, School Board Meeting Notes, December 2, 1940.

55   Caroline County Public Schools, School Board Meeting Notes, July 1, 1941.

56   Caroline County Public Schools, School Board Meeting Notes, August 4, 1942.

57   Caroline County Public Schools, School Board Meeting Notes, September 7, 1942.

58   *Free Lance Star* January 26, 1946 Urges Extensive Plan for Improving Schools page 1.

59   Caroline County Public Schools, School Board Meeting Notes, November 5, 1945.

60   "Caroline County Boards Planning Action on Budgets," *Free Lance Star*, March 9, 1950, 2.

61   "Combining of Gym and Auditorium In School Opposed," *Free Lance Star*, November 24, 1950, 5.

62   Union High 1957 Yearbook. "Union School Addition is Formally Accepted," *Free Lance Star*, January 4, 1961, 3. "Caroline School Board Appoints Building Aide," *Free Lance Star*, February 5, 1964, 2.

63   "Aims and Objectives of the Social Students Department of Union High School," Aims and Objectives of the Various Departments of Union High, 1964–1965.

64   "Industrial Arts and Masonry Objectives," *Aims and Objectives of the Various Departments of Union High, 1964–1965*.

65   Industrial Arts and Masonry Objectives, *Aims and Objectives of the Various Departments of Union High, 1964–1965*.

66   Industrial Arts and Masonry Objectives, *Aims and Objectives of the Various Departments of Union High, 1964–1965*.

67   Music Department Objectives, *Aims and Objectives of the Various Departments of Union High, 1964–1965*.

68   "School Board Asked to Study UHS Program," *Free Lance Star*, October 8.

69   Bryant, 112.

70   Bryant, 113–114.

71   Bryant, 116.

72   History of Union High's Home Economics Department, The Papers of Archie Richardson.

73   Superintendent of Public Instruction of the Commonwealth of Virginia, *Annual Report of the Superintendent of Public Instruction of the Commonwealth of Virginia with Accompanying Documents, School Year 1936 – 1937*, 32.

74   Bryant, 115–116

75   VIA Handbook August 19, 1964, 3.

76   Bryant, 115–116.

77   Union High 1958 Yearbook.

78   History of Union High's Home Economics Department, The Papers of Archie G. Richardson 1918–1976 in the Special Collections and Archives of the Johnston Memorial Library of Virginia State University.

79   Union High 1958 Yearbook.

80   Union High School, Catalogue, 1930–1931, 6.

81   Helaine Patterson, "Broken Bat, Mitt Were Start," *Free Lance Star*, January 28, 1971.

82   Kurt Nicoll, "Minor got a major shot," *Free Lance Star*, February 8, 2004.

83   Kurt Nicoll, "Lowe Built Baseball Legacy," *Free Lance Star*, April 17, 2005.

84   Caroline County Public Schools, School Board Meeting Notes, January 1, 1944.

85   Caroline County Public Schools, School Board Meeting Notes, February 26, 1965.

86   "Caroline Drafts Plan to Drop Racial Bars," *Free Lance Star*, May 4, 1965, 1.

87   Thomas Mann, "Caroline County School Plan Gets Federal Government OK," *Free Lance Star*, October 19, 1965, 6.

88   U.S. District Court Case no. was 5951-R.

89   "Caroline Names in School Suite," *Free Lance Star*, August 29, 1968.

90   "Two Desegregation Plans Offered," *Free Lance Star*, February 5, 1969, 15.

91   Helaine Patterson, "Rural Caroline County School Is Boycotted by Whites," *Free Lance Star*, September 3, 1969, 1.

92   Rusty Dennen and Paul Sullivan, "Integration brought alternative academies," *Free Lance Star*, June 11, 1980, 1.

93   History of the Sunday School Union (author and date unknown).

94   Union High Memorial Committee Members: Dr. Walter E. Lowe, Chairman, Mrs. LaVerne Carter, Mrs. Doris Carter, Mrs. Paulette Davis, Mrs. Arletha Rucker, Mrs. Blanche Washington, Rev. Walter T. Young, Rev. Wendell N. Sims, Mr. Lawrence Golden (inactive), and Mr. John Golden (inactive)

95   Jim Crow was a minstrel character popularized during the 1830s. The character was portrayed by a white man in black face who sang and danced in an exaggerated manner and reinforced all the negative stereotypes about Negroes. The character and minstrel shows helped to popularize the belief that Negroes were lazy, stupid, and inferior to Whites. The phrase Jim Crow later was used to describe laws and customs that oppressed Negroes during the era of segregation.

96   County training schools and public secondary education for Negroes in the South (1935), 31.

Bibliography

MANUSCRIPT AND ARCHIVAL COLLECTIONS

The Archie G. Richardson Papers, Accession #1997-77, Special Collections and Archives, Johnston Memorial Library, Virginia State University, Petersburg, Virginia.

The Hampton University Archives, Hampton University Museum, Hampton University, Hampton, Virginia.

Jackson Davis Collection of African American Educational Photographs, Special Collections, University of Virginia Library

The Luther Porter Jackson Papers, 1772-1960 Special Collections and Archives, Johnston Memorial Library, Virginia State University Collection Number 1952-1

Virginia Intercollegiate Association Papers 1969-37, Special Collections and Archives, Johnston Memorial Library, Virginia State University, Petersburg, Virginia.

The Virginia State Teachers Association Papers, Accession #1969-14, Special Collections and Archives, Johnston Memorial Library, Virginia State University, Petersburg, Virginia.

BOOKS

Bryant, Florence C. *Memoirs of a Country Girl*. New York: Vantage Press, 1988.

Braeman, John, Robert H. Bremner, and David Brody. 1975. *The New Deal Vol.2, The State and Local Levels*. Columbus: Ohio State University Press.

Caldwell, A. B. *History of the American Negro and His Institutions*, Atlanta, Georgia: A.B. Caldwell Pub. Co.1917.

Coleman, Arcia L. "'Tell the Court I Love My [Indian] Wife': Interrogating Race and Self—Identity in Loving v. Virginia" *Racializing Justice, Disenfranchising Lives: the Racism, Criminal Justice, and Law Reader*. Eds. Manning Marable, Ian Steinberg, and Keesha Middlemass. New York: Palgrave Macmillan, 2007.

Catalogue of the Bowling Green Industrial Academy, 1905–1906, Bowling Green, Virginia, n.d.

Fairclough, Adam. *A Class of Their Own: Black Teachers in the Segregated South*. Cambridge, Mass: Belknap Press of Harvard University Press, 2007.

Redcay, Edward E. *County Training Schools and Public Secondary Education for Negroes in the South (1935)*. Washington, D.C.: John F. Slater Fund, 1935. *Internet Archive*. 31 Oct. 2008. Web. 31 Oct. 2009. <http://www.archive.org/details/countytrainingsc00redcrich>.

———. *Public Secondary Schools for Negroes in the Southern States of the United States;*. Washington, D.C.: John F Slater Fund, 1935. *Internet Archive*. Web. 10 Jan. 2009. <http://www.archive.org/details/publicsecondarys00redc>.

Rountree, Helen C. *Pocahontas's People: the Powhatan Indians of Virginia through Four Centuries*. The Civilization of the American Indian series, [v. 196]. Norman: University of Oklahoma Press, 1990.

Russell, Lester F. *Black Baptist Secondary Schools in Virginia, 1887–1957: A Study in Black History*. Metuchen, N.J.: Scarecrow Press, 1981.

The Negro Problem: A Series of Articles By Representative American Negroes of To-Day. James Pott & Company: New York, 1903.

Union High School. *Catalogue*. Bowling Green, Virginia: Union High School, 1930–1931.

Williams, Juan. *Eyes on the Prize: America's Civil Rights Years, 1954–1965*. New York, N.Y.: Viking, 1987.

Womble, Charles W. *The VIA Story: a Short History of the Virginia Interscholastic Association, 1954–1969*. Petersburg: Virginia State College, 1974.

NEWSPAPERS AND PERIODICALS

"Back to Campus–But in New Roles." *Free Lance Star* [Fredericksburg, Virginia] 10 Jul 1969: 20 Google News, Web. 19 July 2010.

Bolton, Steven. "Not all History Found in Books." *Caroline Progress* [Bowling Green, Virginia] 26 Aug 1987: 1.

"Caroline County Boards Planning Action on Budgets." *Free Lance Star* [Fredericksburg, Virginia] 9 Mar 1950: 2.

"Caroline County To Begin Classes in New Union High." *Free Lance Star* [Fredericksburg, Virginia] 23 Jan 1952: 1.

"Caroline Integration Plan Runs Into Snag." *Free Lance Star* [Fredericksburg, Virginia] 26 Feb 1969: 13.

"Caroline Named in School Suit." *Free Lance Star* [Fredericksburg, Virginia] 29 Aug 1969: 4.

"Caroline School Board Approves Budget, Refuses to Make Public." *Free Lance Star* [Fredericksburg, Virginia] 9 Apr 1969: 9.

"Combining of Gym and Auditorium In School Opposed." *Free Lance Star* [Fredericksburg, Virginia] 24 Nov 1950: 5.

"County Asks Week Delay On Schools." *Free Lance Star* [Fredericksburg, Virginia] 21 Jan 1969: 9.

Dennen , Rusty and Paul Sullivan, "Integration brought alternative academies," *The Free Lance Star* [Fredericksburg, Virginia] June 11, 1980: 1.

"Desegregation Transition Plan Okayed in Caroline." *Free Lance Star* [Fredericksburg, Virginia] 13 Feb 1969: 13.

The Educational Journal [Bowling Green, Virginia] Jan 1904 Vol 1. No.1

Goolrock, John C. "Schools Ready Expansion, Repair Jobs for Openings" *Free Lance Star* [Fredericksburg, Virginia] 29 August 1960: 7.

Hedelt, Rob. "A Different Kind of Graduate." *Free Lance Star* [Fredericksburg] 24 Apr 1979: 1+. Google News. Web. 26 June 2010.

"Hew Threatens School Fund Cutoff." *Free Lance Star* [Fredericksburg, Virginia] 20 Nov 1969: 13.

Lakeman, William. "County May Hold 2nd Registration." *Free Lance Star* [Fredericksburg, Virginia] 24 August 1965: 3.

Lowe, Fraulein. "VSU Alumni Honor Mary Banks." *The Caroline Progress* [Bowling Green, Virginia] 30 Apr 1986: 3.

"Lloyd Boxley Retiring after 37 Years." *The Caroline Progress* [Bowling Green, Virginia] 6 June 1984: 12.

Mann, Thomas. "Caroline County School Plan Gets Federal Government OK." *Free Lance Star* [Fredericksburg, Virginia] 19 October 1965: 6.

Patterson, Helaine. "Caroline Desegregation Plan Outlined." *Free Lance Star* [Fredericksburg, Virginia] 7 Aug 1969: 11.

———. "Caroline Schools Renamed." *Free Lance Star* [Fredericksburg, Virginia] 9 July 1969: 28. Print.

———. "Rural Caroline County School Is Boycotted By Whites." *Free Lance Star* [Fredericksburg, Virginia] 3 Sep 1969: 1.

Ragland, Evelyn P. "Tribute to Mrs. Mary Black Banks '28, '36." *Virginia State University: A Magazine for Alumni and Friends* Summer 2005: 21. *Scrib.* 27 Feb. 2010. Web. 24 Jan. 2010. <http://www.scribd.com/doc/27583796/Virginia-State-University>.

"Retired Caroline Teacher Wins Va. State Alumni Award." *Free Lance Star* [Fredericksburg, Virginia] 4 June 1980: 24.

Ruffin, George B. "Accreditation," *The Pointer Review* (June 1967): 4.

Schermerhorn, Will. "Lloyd Boxley–Retiring after 37 years." *Caroline Progress*, June 6, 1984, 12.

"School Plan Ruling Deferred." *Free Lance Star* [Fredericksburg, Virginia] 24 Jun 1969: 9.

"Students Dedicate 1971 'Profile' To Mary B. Banks." *The Caroline Progress* [Bowling Green, Virginia] 12 May 1971: 11.

"Supervisors Okay School Loan, Clarify Firecracker Law Intent." *Free Lance Star* [Fredericksburg, Virginia] 7 Jun 1969, 3.

"Two Desegregation Plans Offered." *Free Lance Star* [Fredericksburg, Virginia] 5 Feb 1969: 15.

"Two 'Indians' Are Convicted Refused Designation as Colored for Army." *Baltimore Afro-American* [Baltimore] 1 Aug. 1944: 1–2. *Google News*. Web. 2 Apr. 2010.

"Union School Addition Is Formally Accepted." *Free Lance Star* [Fredericksburg, Virginia] 4 Jan 1961: 3.

"Urges Extensive Plan for Improving Schools." *Free Lance Star* January 26, 1946: 1.

"Virginia Teacher Asks Equal Salary Scale," *The Crisis*, December 1938.

Young, Rev. R. W., ed. *The Educational Journal* Vol. 1, No. 1 (Jan. 1904): 1.

GOVERNMENT PUBLICATIONS

Battle, Gilbert C. Jr. Notes from Caroline County Public Schools School Board Meeting, June 10, 1993.

Second Annual Report of the State Commission of Virginia for Year Ending December 31, 1904.

State Board of Education. *Annual Report of the Superintendent of Public Instruction of the Commonwealth of Virginia, School Years 1918–1919 and 1919–1920, Vol. 3, No.4*, Richmond, Virginia: Division of Purchase and Printing, 1921.

———. *Annual Report of the Superintendent of Public Instruction of the Commonwealth of Virginia, School Year 1928–1929, Vol. XII, No.3*, Richmond, Virginia.: Division of Purchase and Printing, 1929.

———. *Annual Report of the Superintendent of Public Instruction of the Commonwealth of Virginia, School Year 1929–1930, Vol. XIII, No.2*, Richmond, Virginia: Division of Purchase and Printing, 1930.

———. *Annual Report of the Superintendent of Public Instruction of the Commonwealth of Virginia, School Year 1930–1931, Vol. XIV, No.3*, Richmond, Virginia: Division of Purchase and Printing, 1932.

Superintendent of Public Instruction of the Commonwealth of Virginia. *Annual Report of the Superintendent of Public Instruction of the Commonwealth of Virginia with Accompanying Documents, School Year 1936–1937.* Richmond, Virginia: Virginia Department of Education, 1937.

———. *Annual Report of the Superintendent of Public Instruction of the Commonwealth of Virginia, with Accompanying Documents.* Richmond, Virginia: Virginia Department of Education, 1969–1970.

U.S. Department of the Interior, Bureau of Education. *Negro Education: A Study of the Private and Higher Schools for Colored People in the United States.* Bulletin, 1916, No. 39, Vol. II, Washington, D.C.: U.S. Government Printing Office, 1917. http://books.google.com/ (accessed January 29, 2009).

The General Education Board An Account of its Activities 1902–1914. New York: General Education Board, 1915. *Internet Archive.* Web. 17 Feb. 2009. <http://www.archive.org/details/generaleducation00geneiala>.

INTERVIEWS AND MEMORY SUBMISSIONS

Adams, Patricia Sizer. Telephone interview by author. March 19, 2010.

Armistead, Lottie Turner. Telephone interview by author. June 21, 2010.

Beverly, Reginald Arthur. Telephone interview by author. Interviewed several times between September 30, 2009, and July 10, 2010.

Black, Dorothy Carter. Telephone interview by author. June 23, 2010.

Boxley, Pauline Shelton. Telephone interview by author. Interviewed multiple times between November 2, 2009 and March 28, 2011.

Brawner, William. Telephone interview by author. February 1, 2010.

Britton, Yvonne Woolfolk. Telephone interview by author. October 21, 2009.

Brown, Aterita Baker. Telephone interview by author. January 8, 2010.

Brown, Cassandra Marie Davis. Telephone interview by author. Interviewed several times between December 26, 2008 and April 21, 2009.

Budd, Judith Jones. Memory submission. March 25, 2011.

Burnett, Diane Boxley. Memory submission. 22 March 2011.

Carter, Laverne Bates. Telephone interview by author. August 12, 2010.

Carter, Wesley T. Interview, Richmond, Virginia. August 15, 2010.

Coleman, Lucille Howard. Telephone interview by author. July 7, 2010.

Coleman, Vivian Garnett. Telephone interview by author. March 5, 2010.

Collins, Beulah. Telephone interview by author. July 8, 2010.

Crump, Joyce "Judy" Brown. Telephone interview by author. June 29, 2010.

Davis, Paulette Sizer. Telephone interview by author. March 15, 2010.

Davis, Thomas. Telephone interview by author. February 17, 2010.

Davis, Williabell Jones. Telephone interview by author. April 28, 2010.

Deyo, Boyd. Telephone interview by author. June 8, 2010.

Dobbins Joseph. Telephone interview by author. March 11, 2010.

Epps, Carolyn Garnett. Telephone interview by author. May 5, 2010.

Ferguson, Catherine. Telephone interview by author. February 19, 2010, and July 23, 2010.

Ferguson, Gladys Rich. Telephone interview by author. March 11, 2010.

Fields, Irene Quash. Telephone interview by author. February 14, 2010, March 7, 2010 and March 13, 2010.

Fitzhugh-Pemberton, Gladys. Telephone interview by author. February 7, 2010.

Freeman, Bernard. Memory submission. March 20, 2011.

Frenzley, Vernelle Bates. Telephone interview by author. July 27, 2010.

Garnett, William Jr. Telephone interview by author. May 3, 2010.

Gill, Katrina Beverly. Memory submission. March 31, 2011.

Gray, Charles. Telephone interview by author. June 22, 2010.

Gray, Rudolph. Telephone interview by author. February 18, 2010.

Harley, Nina Woolfolk. Telephone interview by author. March 3, 2010.

Harris, Clara Sizer. Telephone interview by author. December 10, 2010.

Harris, Regena Green. Telephone interview by author. March 6, 2010.

Hawkins, Eleanor Thomas. Telephone interview by author. July 26, 2010.

Gwathmey, Lavern Baylor. Telephone interview by author. February 12, 2010.

Hudson, Clara Latney. Telephone interview by author. October, 17 2009

Jackson, Arthur. Telephone interview by author. February 25, 2009.

Jackson, Beryl. Telephone interview by author. February 2, 2010.

Jackson, Carolyn. Telephone interview by author. February 25, 2010.

Jackson, Jesse. Telephone interview by author. June 24, 2010.

Jackson, Dorothy Samuels. Telephone interview by author. Jul 20, 2010.

Jackson, Marguerite Davis. Telephone interview by author. Interviewed multiple times between January 16, 2010, and April 18, 2010.

Mary, Jeter. Telephone interview by author. June 12, 2010.

Johnson, Carolyn Bundy. Telephone interview by author. June 29, 2010.

Johnson, Elmer. Telephone interview by author. July 29, 2010.

Johnson, James. Memory submission. March 6, 2011.

Jones, Stanley O. Memory submission. March 18, 2011.

Latney, Oliver Jr. Telephone interview by author. March 26, 2010.

Latney, Virginia Gray. Telephone interview by author. February 5, 2010.

Lee, Jeanetta Rock. Telephone interview by author. November 10, 2009.

Lee, Nancie Gray. Telephone interview by author. September 14, 2010.

Lowe, Walter. Telephone interview by author. Interviewed multiple times between January 2, 2010, and August 8, 2010.

Luck, Ola R. Telephone interview by author. June 13, 2010.

McLean, Nona McReynolds. Telephone interview by author. February 26, 2010.

McReynolds, Ivone Parker. Telephone interview by author. June 17, 2010.

Mickens, Alma Thomas. Telephone interview by author. January 18, 2010.

Miller, Vergie. Telephone interview by author. January 16, 2010.

Minor, Evelyn Thomas. Telephone interview by author. January 12, 2011.

Minor, Waverly. Telephone interview by author. July 27, 2010.

Nichols, Bert Twiggs. Telephone interview by author. December 11, 2010.

Monte, John Jr. Telephone interview by author. January 16, 2010.

Paige, Kenneth. Telephone interview by author. January 18, 2010.

Peatross, Margie. Memory Submission. November 4, 2009.

Quash, Rosa Bell Courtney. Telephone interview by author. January 20, 2010.

Quash, Susie Carter. Telephone interview by author. February 13, 2010.

Ragland, Evelyn. Telephone interview by author. January 18, 2010.

Rock, Barbara Jones. Telephone interview by author. February 11, 2010.

Rollins, Claudia Beverly. Memory submission. March 31, 2011.

Reynolds, Gloria Woodfolk. Telephone interview by author. November 9, 2009.

Robinson, Lorenza Young. Telephone interview by author. January 20, 2010.

Rhue, Florence Lee. Telephone interview by author. July 1, 2010.

Samuels, Kate Hutchinson. Telephone interview by author. [month and day unknown] 2010.

Saunders, Carrie Myers. Telephone interview by author. January 2, 1010.

Silver, Sherrillyn LaVerne Smith. Telephone interview by author. July 13, 2010.

Sizer, Arthur Jr. Telephone interview by author. April 2, 2010, April 27, 2010 and July 19, 2010.

Sizer, Lillian Richardson. Telephone interview by author. March 19, 2010.

Spencer, Joyce Woolfolk. Telephone interview by author. July 8, 2010.

Taylor, Calvin Sr. Telephone interview by author. February 22, 2009.

Thomas, Daisy Jackson. Telephone interview by author. February 15, 2010.

Thomas, Warren. Telephone interview by author. August 23, 2010.

Thompson, Evelyn Wright. Telephone interview by author. March 2, 2010.

Thompson, Geneva Johnson. Telephone interview by author. July 15, 2010.

Thornton, Anna Marie Gray. Telephone interview by author. February 20, 2010.

Tipton, Blonnie. Telephone interview by author. June 22, 2010.

Twiggs, Shirley Johnson. Telephone interview by author. January 11, 2010

Twiggs, Shirley Vernelle. Telephone interview by author. January 20, 2010.

Underwood, Vera Twiggs. Telephone interview by author. February 23, 2010.

Upshaw, Morton. Telephone interview by author. February 16, 2010.

Vaughan, Emma Samuel. Telephone interview by author, July 28, 2010.

Washington, Blanch Lomax. Telephone interview by author. February 2, 2010.

Washington, Marshall E. Memory submission. March 20, 2011.

Washington, Oliver. Interview by author, Bowling Green, Virginia. September 19, 2009.

Woodfork, Charles. Telephone interview by author. June 30, 2010.

Woolfolk. Rogers. Memory submission. March 15, 2011.

Young, Louise Boone. Interview Bowling Green, Virginia. August 14, 2010.

Young, Walter. Telephone interview by author. September 26, 2009, February 16, 2010 and July 12, 2011.

UNPUBLISHED THESES AND DISSERTATIONS

Collins, Lewis G. "Educational Development of Caroline County Virginia, 1870–1940." Dissertation. George Washington University, 1941.

Lowe, Walter E. "A Study of the Relationship Between the Socio-Economic Status and the Reading Performance of Negro Students Enrolled in the Public Schools of Caroline County, Virginia." Dissertation. George Washington University, 1969.

WEBSITES

"The Civil Rights Movement in Virginia—Virginia Historical Society." *Virginia Historical Society—The Center for Virginia History*. Web. 25 Oct. 2009. <http://www.vahistorical.org/civilrights/main.htm>.

Fisk University Rosenwald Fund Card File Database (http://rosenwald.fisk.edu/).

Linda B. Pincham, "A League of Willing Workers: The Impact of Northern Philanthropy, Virginia Estelle Randolph and the Jeanes Teachers in Early Twentieth-Century Virginia," *The Journal of Negro Education* 74:2 (Spring, 2005), 112–123.

DEEDS

Caroline County Circuit Court, Deed Book 67:158, Bowling Green, Virginia.

———, Deed Book 67:140, Bowling Green, Virginia.

———, Deed Book 69:7, Bowling Green, Virginia.

———, Deed Book 71:373, Bowling Green, Virginia.

———, Deed Book 76:66, Bowling Green, Virginia.

———, Deed Book, Deed Book 84:607, Bowling Green, Virginia.

Some of the photos in this book were restored by pixlfixl.com.

To find out about having your treasured but time-worn photos digitally restored, please contact Drew Klausner at (415) 456-3221 or go to www.pixlfixl.com.

Before

After